APACHEANS BEARING GIFTS:
PREHISPANIC INFLUENCE ON THE PUEBLO INDIANS

Stuart J. Baldwin

Department of Anthropology
Lakehead University
955 Oliver Road
Thunder Bay, Ontario
Canada   P7B 5E1

February 1997

The Arizona Archaeologist

February 1997   Number 29

This printing of *Arizona Archaeologist Number 29* is a facsimile of the original 1997 publication, digitally scanned in February 2014 for publication. No changes have been made to the text.

The cover drawing is taken from a 1944 photograph by John C. Ewers of a Blackfoot cloth tipi cover (Glenbow Museum photographic archives NA-3324-2, Calgary). It depicts a bear with a heartline, kidneys and jointmarks; see page 34 for discussion. Drawing by Ron Beckwith.

ISBN 0939071320

Published by the Arizona Archaeological Society, Inc.

P.O. Box 9665

Phoenix, AZ 85068-9665

www.AzArchSoc.org

Members of the Arizona Archaeological Society, at the time of publication, have the option of receiving either a free hardcopy or PDF version of the *Arizona Archaeologist*. PDF versions of most previous editions are available to members at any time on the "Members Only" page of the Society's website.

TABLE OF CONTENTS

LIST OF FIGURES

ACKNOWLEDGMENTS

The research for this study was conducted without formal funding. I wish to thank Dr. Alan Bryan for access to unpublished information. Also Sally Cole, David Wilcox and R.G. Matson for discussion and comment on some aspects of my presentation of some of this material at the 1992 Chacmool Conference in Calgary. And, finally, to Alan Ferg, David Wilcox, and the AAS's anonymous reviewers for their comments on the submitted manuscript.

ABSTRACT

This study proposes that Apacheans immigrating into the Southwest from the Northern Great Plains introduced a complex of cultural traits associated with hunting and warfare to the Pueblo Indians before the arrival of the first Spanish explorers. This hunting-warfare complex consists of three artifact types - (1) the sinew-backed bow, (2) the mountain lion-skin quiver, and (3) the bison-hide shield - and two motifs that appear in rock art and on artifacts - (4) the four-pointed star, and (5) the heartline.

Examination of archaeological evidence from the Southwest indicates a lack of the five traits prior to the beginning of the Pueblo IV period, around A.D. 1300. Earliest datable appearances of each of the five traits within the Southwest are found to be within the A.D. 1400s, concurrent with the probable time of arrival of the Apacheans.

Additional archaeological data indicate that all five traits can be traced back to the Northern Great Plains, and the heartline motif to possible origins somewhere on the northeastern periphery of the Great Plains. Finally, a tentative reconstruction of a two-stage migration south by the Apacheans from Alberta to New Mexico is presented.

1

THE APACHEANS

The term Apacheans refers to the Athapaskan-speaking peoples who separated from the main mass of Athapaskans inhabiting the Western Subarctic culture area, migrated south to the Southwest culture area, and there differentiated into the Navajo and various Apache groups. Over the years considerable discussion and divergence of opinion has occurred concerning the specific migration route(s) of the Apacheans and the time(s) of their arrival in the Southwest (see Wilcox 1981). I have always favored a migration route south from southern Alberta to northeastern New Mexico along the eastern foothills of the Rocky Mountains, with concurrent use of plains and mountain environments to the east and west. This is based upon the earliest historically-known locations for the Apacheans: in northeastern New Mexico, the Texas and Oklahoma panhandles, eastern Colorado and extreme western Kansas (Figure 1). Note that I do not accept Forbes' (1959) contention that various Southern Plains-North Mexican groups such as the Jumanos, Mansos, Sumas and others were Athapaskans.

The earliest Spanish descriptions of Apachean culture (from A.D. 1541) depict a plains-adapted lifestyle: a nomadic, bison-hunting people, utilizing tanned bison hides for clothing and tipi covers, conversant in sign language, using pack-dogs for carrying their possessions and dragging tipi poles, and trading with horticultural peoples such as the Pueblo Indians and the Wichita (Baldwin 1988b:121-124).

The time of their earliest arrival is unclear at present. For southeastern Colorado, Kingsbury and Gabel (1983) attribute tipi rings radiocarbon dated to A.D. 1350 ± 55 to the Apacheans. Recent evidence from the Texas panhandle correlates the Apacheans with the Tierra Blanca complex that dates at least as early as A.D. 1450 (Habicht-Mauche 1992). And recently the concept of a Dinetah Phase in the traditional Navajo homeland (the *Dinetááh*) in Northern New Mexico, beginning perhaps as early as A.D. 1350, has been revived by Hogan (1989) and Reed and Horn (1990). R.G. Matson (verbal communication 1992) has observed that there exist unpublished criticisms of at least some of the dates used by Reed and Horn (1990) to establish a relatively early occupation of the *Dinetááh* area.

I tentatively accept an arrival of the Apacheans in southeastern Colorado between A.D. 1350 and 1400, with an immediate farther spread south into New Mexico and Texas. Hence,

I suggest an Apachean impact upon the Pueblo Indians of north-central New Mexico beginning ca. A.D. 1400.

Within this temporal context I suggest that the Pueblo Indians quickly adopted a hunting-warfare complex from the newly arrived Apacheans. This complex included the following elements:

1. The sinew-backed bow,
2. The mountain lion-skin quiver,
3. The bison-hide shield,
4. The four-pointed star motif, and
5. The heartline motif.

The evidence for Apachean introduction of each of these elements is discussed next.

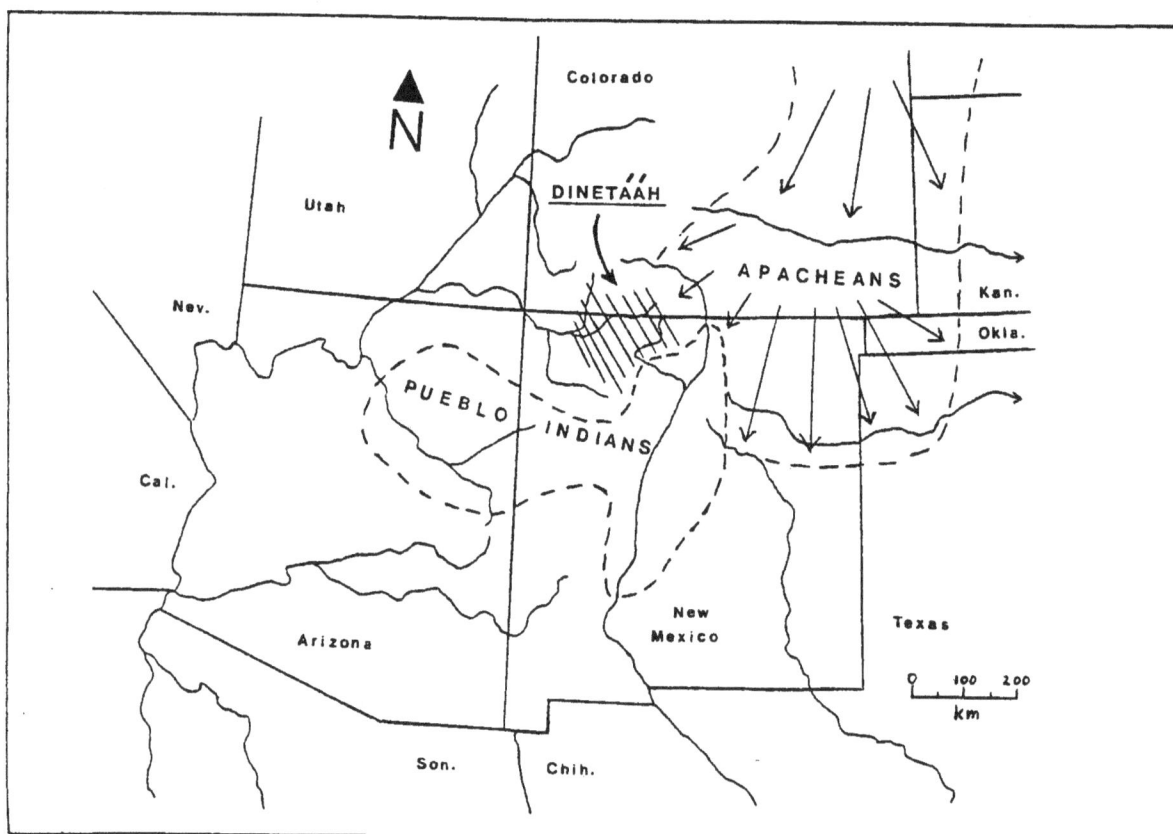

Figure 1. Map showing Pueblo Indian area of occupation during early Pueblo IV (ca. A.D. 1300-1500), Apachean zone of occupation on Southern Plains (ca. A.D. 1350-1540), and *Dinetááh* homeland of Navajo.

2

THE SINEW-BACKED BOW

It has previously been suggested that the Pueblo Indians obtained the sinew-backed bow from Apachean sources (Underhill 1944:108; Brugge 1983:109-110). However, the evidence for this diffusion event has not been summarized previously: that is the purpose of this section.

Aboriginal New World bow technology achieved three basic levels of development: the self-bow, the sinew-backed bow, and the composite bow. The self-bow is composed of a single piece of wood plus the bowstring; its cast (throwing distance) is mainly dependent on the quality of the wood. The sinew-backed bow is the self-bow plus thin layers of sinew glued onto its back (the surface facing away from the archer). Once the applied sinew dries, it produces a higher tension, hence a greater cast, than can be achieved by most self-bows. The composite bow as made in North America consists of two parallel pieces of material: a belly piece of antler or mountain sheep horn and a back piece of thick sinew and glue. This produces an even more powerful cast than the sinew-backed bow (Hamilton 1982:2-11; McEwen *et al.* 1991:79-81).

ETHNOGRAPHIC BOW USE

The self-bow was in almost universal use in the New World at the time of first European contact. The sinew-backed bow was of more limited distribution: mainly confined to the California, Southwest, Great Basin, and Plateau culture areas, and to the western portions of the Great Plains (Driver and Massey 1957:349-352). The composite bow was a very late invention, perhaps as late as A.D. 1700 (Hamilton 1982:9), and was limited in production to native groups in the Plateau culture area and perhaps some adjacent groups of the Northern Plains.

Within the Southwest, ethnographic data show the sinew-backed bow to be limited in production and use to the Pueblo Indians, the Navajo, and the various Apache groups (Gifford 1940:29-30; Kluckhohn *et al.* 1971:23-29; Underhill 1944:110-111), and lacking among Yuman-speakers and the Pimas and other Uto-Aztecan-speakers of southern Arizona and northern Mexico (Drucker 1941:118; Driver and Massey 1957:352).

The early historical records provided by the Spaniards are very incomplete regarding ethnographic details, but the reports of "Turkish bows" among the Pueblo Indians during the A.D. 1580s are almost certainly references to sinew-backed bows, as is discussed in Hamilton (1982:64-66). Later explorers from the United States gave better descriptions, such as this excellent one of Apache bows provided by Zebulon Pike (in Coues 1987:749) from A.D. 1806:

> Their bow forms two demi-circles, with a shoulder in the middle; the back of it is entirely covered with sinews, which are laid on in so nice a manner, by use of some glutinous substance, as to be almost imperceptible; this gives great elasticity to the weapon.

Given that both Pueblo Indians and Apacheans are documented historically and ethnographically to have the sinew-backed bow, it remains to establish its time and manner of introduction.

PREHISTORIC BOW USE

Archaeological evidence documents the presence of only the self-bow in the Southwest before A.D. 1300. This evidence consists of (1) the actual remains of wooden bows from dry rockshelters and other sites, and (2) the depiction of hunters and warriors using a D-shaped bow on painted ceramics or in datable rock art. I do not have a precise count of how many prehistoric bows have been recovered archaeologically in the Southwest, but it is substantial given that a single cache of bows from the Mogollon Mountains produced over 90 specimens (Hibben 1938). The critical point is that *all* of these are self-bows.

The self-bow is characteristically D-shaped (see Figure 2), and all pre-A.D. 1300 depictions of bows in the Southwest have this shape (see Figure 3), except for some where the shape is more of a pointed oval - indicating that the bowstring is being drawn back by the archer. Painted depictions of bows on ceramic vessels are found on Anasazi pottery from Mesa Verde during Pueblo I and Pueblo III (A.D. 700-900 and 1100-1300), on Mogollon pottery from the Mimbres area (A.D. 1000-1150), and on Hohokam pottery at Snaketown during the Gila Butte and Sacaton phases (A.D. 550-700 and 900-1100); for examples see Brody (1991:32), Nordenskiöld (1893:108), Brody *et al.* (1983:72, 96, 98), and Haury (1976:238).

Rock art depictions include both petroglyphs and pictographs that are part of dated rock art styles, specifically the Gila Petroglyph Style (ca. A.D. 200-1300), the Rosa Representational Style (ca. A.D. 600-900), the Virgin Representational Style (ca. A.D. 1000-1150), the Kayenta Representational Style (ca. A.D. 1050-1250), Pueblo II and Pueblo III rock art at Mesa Verde

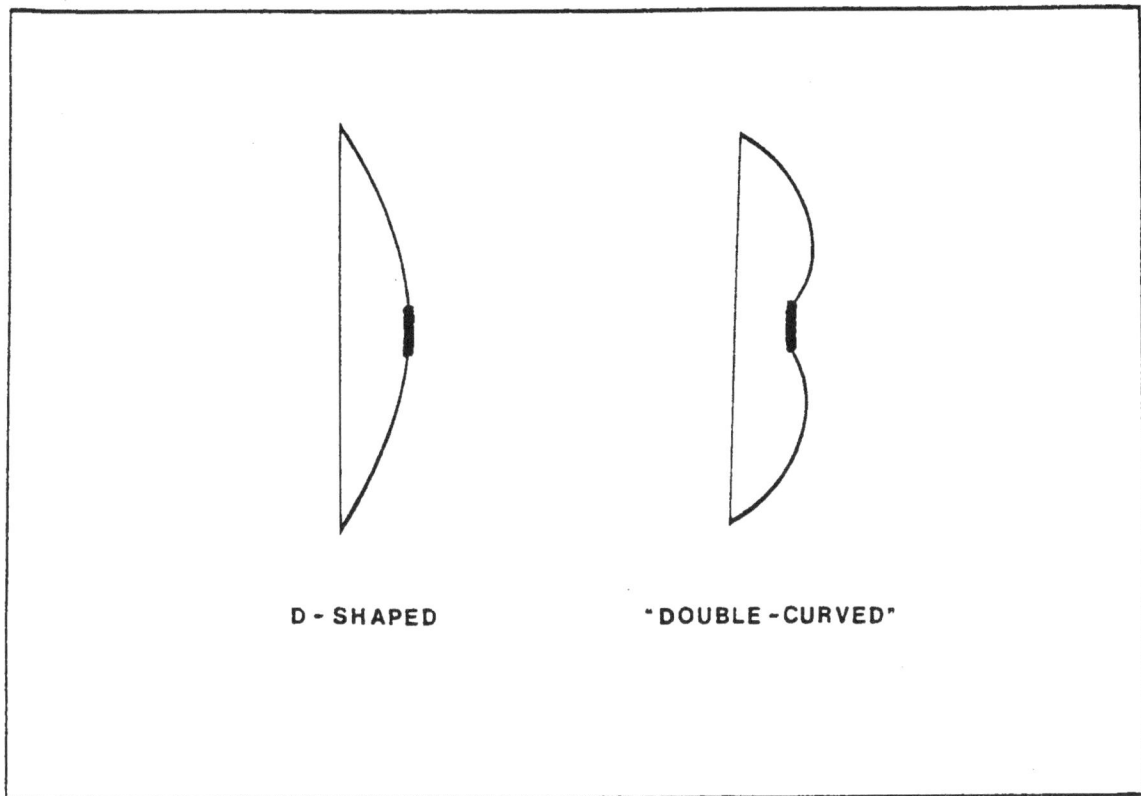

D - SHAPED   "DOUBLE-CURVED"

Figure 2. Basic bow shapes.

Figure 3. Design on
Mimbres Black-on-white
bowl showing quivers,
bows, and arrows.
From Fewkes (1914:27).

and Chaco Canyon (ca. A.D. 900-1300), and the Northern San Rafael Style (ca. A.D. 800-1250) as defined by Schaafsma (1980) and the Candelaria Style (perhaps A.D. 1100-1400) in Northern Chihuahua (Davis 1980). Locations of rock art and ceramic depictions of the self-bow predating A.D. 1300 known to me are shown in Figure 4 and sources listed in Appendix A.

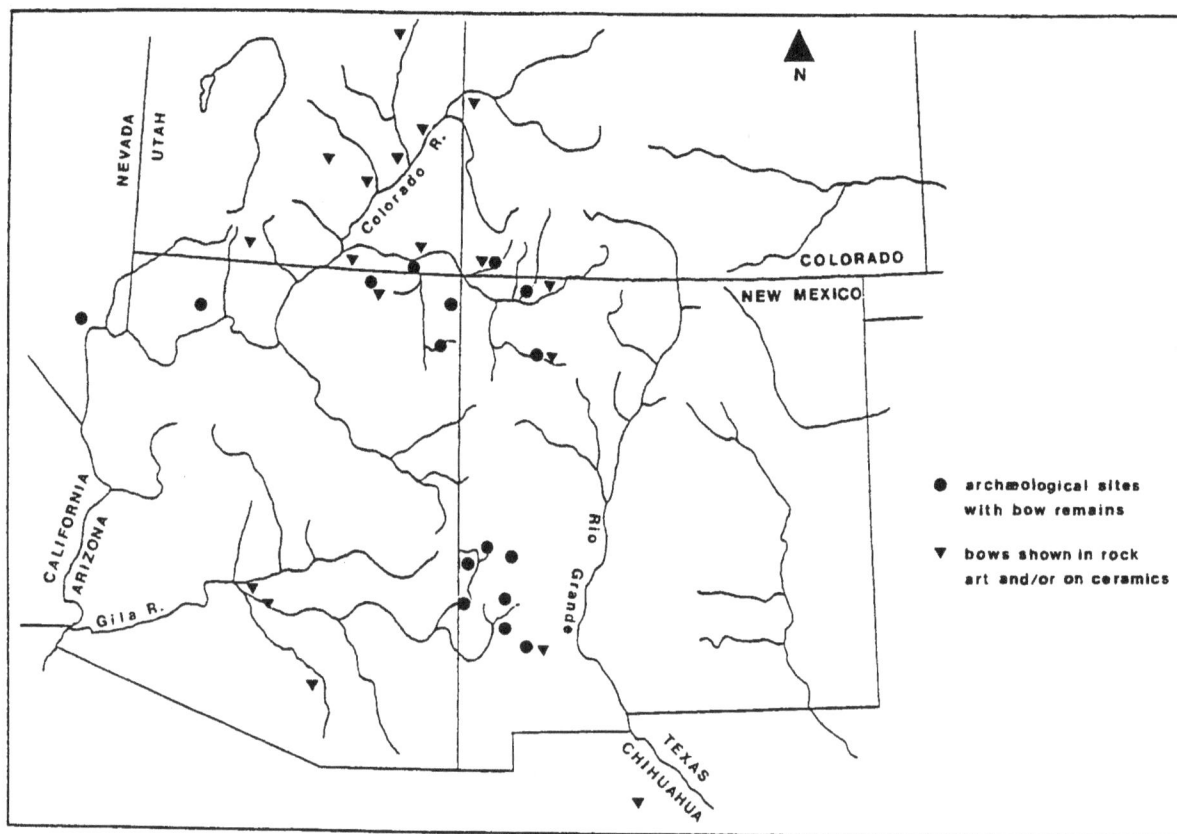

Figure 4. Map showing pre-A.D. 1300 rock art and archaeological sites documenting use of the self-bow in the Southwest. See Appendix A for enumeration of materials found at these sites.

6

THE INTRODUCTION OF THE SINEW-BACKED BOW

The first evidence of a change in bow technology in the Southwest is the appearance of "double-curved" bows in kiva murals and rock art during the Pueblo IV period (A.D. 1300-1700). The "double-curved" shape is characteristic of the sinew-backed bow, just as the D-shape is characteristic of the self-bow (see Figure 2). Both bow shapes are direct responses to the physical forces set up when the bow is "braced", i.e., when the bowstring has been attached to both ends and the bow is ready for use. There is a *caveat*, however: a "double-curved" shape can be induced in a self-bow by intentionally warping the wood and many self-bows made by the Plains Indians and others have this warping. The problem is that this warping of a self-bow produces *no improvement in performance*, hence seems "irrational" from a strictly functional point of view (see discussion in Hamilton 1982:46-47). My speculation is that the "double-curved" self-bow is an attempt to gain the superior performance of the sinew-backed bow by simply copying its shape.

I suggest that the appearance of "double-curved" bow forms in the depictions dating after A.D. 1300 is a symptom of the arrival of the sinew-backed bow technology. Fortunately, it can confidently be said that this was during the early A.D. 1400s since the kiva murals at Pottery Mound that show the "double-curved" bow form (Hibben 1975:44, 46, 68-69, 80) were produced before abandonment of the site, ca. A.D. 1450-1475. Other, less precisely datable, depictions of "double-curved" bows can be found in the kiva murals at Awatovi (Smith 1952:Plate A and Figure 53b) and in the Pueblo IV rock art of Abo Pass and the Pajarito Plateau (Baldwin 1988a:595; Chapman 1938).

It cannot be proved whether the "double-curved" bows shown in these murals and rock art are true sinew-backed bows or just self-bows imitating the shape of sinew-backed bows. However, two of the Pottery Mound murals show "double-curved" bows in profile that are colored brown (presumably the color of the wood), but with a black edging along the backs of the bows (Hibben 1975:44, 80). This black edging brings to mind an interesting description of sinew-backed bows from Laguna Pueblo: "The entire back is covered with strips of sinew, glued on longitudinally and colored black" (Ellis 1959). Normally, the sinews and glue are colorless and difficult to detect (see description by Pike quoted above), but if a black coloring agent was added to the glue, then a black edging like that shown in the murals would result. I suggest that this is what is depicted at Pottery Mound.

It should also be noted that D-shaped bows continue to appear in the kiva murals and rock art, frequently side-by-side with the "double-curved" bows. This fits well with the ethnographic situation, where both the Pueblo Indians and Apacheans continued to make and use the self-bow concurrent with the sinew-backed bow (Underhill 1944:108-111).

Unfortunately, archaeological recovery of bow specimens from post-A.D. 1300 contexts does not assist us at this point: all *described* bow specimens of Pueblo IV date are small ceremonial bows - taking the form of miniature self-bows - that were never intended for hunting or warfare use (e.g., Gifford 1980:92-94). It is reported that full-size, functional bows were found with burials at Hawikuh (Smith *et al.* 1966:222), but none of these are adequately described.

The apparent synchronicity of the Apachean arrival in the Southwest and the appearance of the sinew-backed bow technology is the main arguing point for a transmission of that technology from them to the Pueblo Indians. There is also, however, some evidence from Pueblo Indian traditions: "according to one informant, the sinew-backed bow was introduced at Santa Clara by the Jicarilla Apache - the time was not known" (Hill 1982:112). And there is an Acoma myth (Stirling 1942:96) in which the young Twin Wargods visit their father, the Sun, at a village in the east (where the sun rises) where the inhabitants aid them as follows:

The boys had brought their bows and arrows. So the men [of the Sun's village] took these and improved them. They put sinew backs on the bows and shaped them better. They put arrowheads and feathers on the arrows and made [mountain] lion-skin quivers.

I suggest that the transmittal of the sinew-backed bow technology from Apacheans to Pueblo Indians has been incorporated into this mythical account.

3

THE MOUNTAIN LION-SKIN QUIVER

While quivers can be made from a variety of leathers, animal skins and basketry, there is a marked preference for quivers made from the skin of the mountain lion (*Felis concolor*) among the Apacheans and Pueblo Indians of the Southwest (Gifford 1940:32) and by some ethnic groups of the Great Plains (known groups include the Blackfoot, Cheyenne, Hidatsa, Kiowa, and Pawnee).

Among both Apacheans and Pueblo Indians the mountain lion-skin quiver consisted of an arrow case, a bow case, and a carrying strap all made from the skin, with the tail hanging down from mouth of the arrow case, and a stiffening rod of wood. Even the cutting patterns for the quivers are very similar (Hill 1982:114-115; Kluckhohn *et al.* 1971:46-51; Opler 1941:391, 1983b:Figure 5; Basso 1971:234).

The mountain lion-skin quiver as reported from the Great Plains groups has the same essential components: arrow case, bow case, carrying strap and stiffening rod (Wissler 1910:158-162); and illustrated examples show the tail pendant from the top of the quiver. This close structural similarity suggests a common origin.

While ethnographic data on this point are very incomplete, it seems clear that the spiritual power and mythical associations of the mountain lion are the main basis for its attractiveness as a quiver material (see Grinnell 1972:184; Kluckhohn *et al.* 1971:46-51; Cushing 1883:15). However, a functional basis, the waterproof nature of fur-surfaced quivers, is noted for the Pawnee quivers (Mason 1894:675).

PREHISTORIC EVIDENCE

Archaeological evidence regarding pre-A.D. 1300 quivers in the Southwest is very scanty: (1) Birdsall (1891:599) reports that the Wetherill brothers recovered a buckskin quiver with arrows (no description) from a Pueblo III cliff dwelling at Mesa Verde; (2) Haury (1950:418, 427) reports recovery of a tubular buckskin quiver with arrows of Desert Hohokam origins from Ventana Cave; and (3) there are several depictions of quivers on Mimbres bowls, dating ca. A.D. 1000-1150 (e.g., Fewkes 1914:27; Brody *et al.* 1983:89).

9

The available Mimbres illustrations show what appear to be cylindrical arrow quivers that lack an attached bow case. Carrying straps are also not shown, but this may simply be an artistic omission of an assumed component. There is no evidence of a dangling tail on any of the Mimbres quivers. The two quivers shown in Figure 3 appear to have cords with attached stylized feathers hanging from the bottoms. Referring to the same quivers, the four points projecting from the side of each one may be the legs of an animal skin, like the bobcat skin quiver shown for the ethnographic Pima in Russell (1908:Plate XIIId). I know of only a single rock art representation of a quiver: a petroglyph archer with D-shaped bow and simple, undetailed quiver in Glen Canyon (Turner 1963:Figure 85).

INTRODUCTION OF THE MOUNTAIN LION-SKIN QUIVER

While the archaeological evidence is hardly conclusive as to an absence of the mountain lion-skin quiver before A.D. 1300, the little evidence available does not support its presence. However, it is clearly present in Pueblo IV (A.D. 1300-1700) and after. Here the main evidence consists of kiva mural depictions at Gran Quivira, Pottery Mound, and Awatovi (see Peckham 1981:24; Hibben 1975:69, 110; Smith 1952:Plate A), where the quivers are shown as a yellow arrow case, a dangling yellow tail tipped in white and/or black, and a carrying strap. The lack of a bow case may (or may not) be an artistic convention. The other quivers shown at Awatovi and Pottery Mound come in other colors and/or with shorter tails. Some of these, particularly the blue quivers at Awatovi, may be mythico-religious references to directional color symbolism, such as is definitely seen at Pottery Mound in the depiction of a mountain lion in a non-naturalistic blue color. In other cases the quivers may be made from other materials, such as the sole quiver depicted in the Kuaua murals: a blue, diamond-patterned quiver that be a rattlesnake skin or a basketry pattern (Dutton 1963:frontispiece).

Dating for the kiva mural quivers comes from two sites: (1) Pottery Mound, with its abandonment date of A.D. 1450-1475, suggests a date in the first half of the 1400s; and (2) Kiva N at Gran Quivira, where the quiver appears on Layer 18 out of 31 layers (or, about halfway between the beginning and end of the kiva's use), which was constructed ca. A.D. 1416 and burned and abandoned by A.D. 1500 (Peckham 1981:17). This latter suggests to me an approximate date of A.D. 1450-1460 for the painting of the quiver mural. Combined, these dates indicate an introduction of the mountain lion-skin quiver sometime after A.D. 1400.

Finally, the Acoma myth quoted above with regard to the origin of sinew-backed bows notes that the people living in the east also made mountain lion-skin quivers for the twins, and particularly notes the stiffening rod as part of the quiver (Stirling 1942:96-97). As above, I interpret this as a mythologized memory of the transfer between the Apacheans and the Pueblo Indians.

4

THE BISON-HIDE SHIELD

The third element of the weapons complex is the bison-hide shield. While ethnographic data record that this kind of shield was sometimes made of elk-hide, and more recently of cow-hide or horse-hide, the bulk of the accounts make it clear that the tougher, thicker hide of the bison was the generally preferred material. Historically and ethnographically, the bison-hide shield is closely associated with ethnic groups inhabiting the Great Plains culture area, and secondarily with some groups in the adjacent Southwest, Great Basin, Plateau and Eastern woodlands (see Driver and Massey 1957:362-363; Gifford 1940:32; Stewart 1942:269; Ray 1942:153).

Manufacturing details of the bison-hide shield are very similar from ethnic group to ethnic group, with even variations following similar patterns, which points to a common origin for this technology (see basic descriptions in Hall 1926; Kluckhohn *et al.* 1971:368-372; Opler 1941:391-392; Wright 1976). The shield is a circular to elliptical cut piece of rawhide (sometimes doubled), most commonly from the neck hide of the bison, that is dried and stretched into a convex shape and provided with a leather handle or strap on the interior. While the material of the shield was very tough and effective in performing its protective function, the native groups using it believed that the defensive power of the design painted on the shield's face was more important. This belief was so strong that an attempt by fur traders to sell metal shields to the Northern Plains groups failed due to the lack of individuated protective designs (Bradley 1923:258).

A "round hide shield" is recorded for the Yumans and Pimans of Arizona (Drucker 1941:120), but this kind of shield is structurally different from the bison-hide shield, being made of one or two *flat* disks of deer rawhide with a handle on the back (see Spier 1955:10; Russell 1908:120-122). Another variety consisted of a single flat disk of hide stretched across a wooden hoop (Gifford 1933:275). I consider both kinds to be unrelated to the bison-hide shield under discussion here.

Originally, the shields seem to have been made large enough to cover the whole torso of the warrior, which would require a minimum vertical diameter of 70 to 80 cm for warriors between 1.5 and 1.75 m tall (or 5'0" to 5'9"). Such large shields were used by pedestrian warriors and are shown in prehistoric rock art of the Western Plains from Alberta to New Mexico (see Gebhard 1966; Keyser 1975; Schaafsma 1972:193). It has been argued that the introduction of horses and firearms by Europeans led to abandonment of the large body shield (e.g., Magne and Klassen 1991:410), and Wright (1976:8) claims that a smaller version of the bison-hide shield (typically about 46 cm in diameter) was characteristic of the Great Plains cultures after the introduction of the horse.

While there is some validity to these statements, they may be over-generalizations. For example, while the ethnographer Wissler (1910:163) only notes shields of ca. 49 cm diameter for the Blackfoot, Lieutenant Bradley (1923:258), an American military man with firsthand knowledge of the Blackfoot in the A.D. 1860s, reports shield sizes of "from two to three feet in diameter" (ca. 61 to 91 cm) which suggests the late survival of large shield sizes among at least some groups.

EARLY HISTORICAL EVIDENCE

The earliest historical mention of Pueblo Indian shields was in A.D. 1541, when Hopi and Zuni examples are called by the Spanish term *rodela*, probably meaning a round hide shield (Winship 1896:126, 128). In the 1580s the Spaniards report oval bison-hide shields among the Piro (Baldwin 1988a:113). The Spaniards note hide shields for the Vaquero Apaches of northeastern New Mexico in A.D. 1598 (Baldwin 1988b:129) and large bison-hide body shields are specifically noted for the Escanjaques, a Southern Plains Caddoan group, in A.D. 1601 (Hammond and Rey 1953:841).

PREHISTORIC EVIDENCE

The greatest amount of evidence for shields in the Southwest before A.D. 1300 comes from rock art of the Fremont Culture in Utah, where round shields are shown either covering the whole torso or being held at arm's length beside the warrior. These appear in dated rock art styles: the Classic Vernal Style (ca. A.D. 600-1000) and the Northern and Southern San Rafael Styles (ca. A.D. 700-1250) (Schaafsma 1980:166-176). No archaeological specimens of Fremont shields are known. The famous Pectol Shields from south-central Utah, large bison-hide body shields (Morss 1931:69-70), are radiocarbon dated to ca. A.D. 1650-1750 (Berger and Libby 1968:149), hence are probably of Ute origin.

Evidence for shield use among the Anasazi is limited to Pueblo III (A.D. 1100-1300) in southern Utah, northeastern Arizona, and the adjacent parts of New Mexico and Colorado that are nearest Fremont territory. Hence Schaafsma (1980:171) suggests that rock art depictions of shields in this area resulted from interaction between the Fremont and the Anasazi. Three examples of Anasazi shields are known: (1) an oval basketry body shield (91 x 79 cm) with a wooden handle from a burial at Aztec Ruin, New Mexico (Morris 1924:193-195); (2) a circular basketry body shield (79 cm diameter) from Mummy Cave, Canyon de Chelly, Arizona; and (3) a smaller (48 cm diameter) circular basketry shield from Wetherill Mesa, Mesa Verde, Colorado (Morris and Burgh 1941:51-52). While made of basketry, these shields resemble the later bison-hide shields in their form (circular, convex) and in having designs on their faces. This suggests that the Fremont shields may also have been basketry.

The only other area of the Southwest giving evidence of shield use prior to A.D. 1300 is the Mimbres area of the Mogollon culture, which has yielded a Mimbres Polychrome bowl painted with a warrior holding a spear and a U-shaped body shield (Brody 1977:Plate 14). The material of this shield is not determinable; it would date to between A.D. 1000-1150.

THE INTRODUCTION OF THE BISON-HIDE SHIELD

I correlate the introduction of the bison-hide shield to the Southwest with the increased frequency of shield depictions during Pueblo IV (A.D. 1300-1700). The Pueblo Indian rock art of this period provides many depictions of large, circular, decorated body shields, especially in the Galisteo Basin and Abo Pass, both areas on the frontier with the Southern Plains (see Schaafsma 1972:129-183; Schaafsma 1980:243-299; Baldwin 1988a:597-605). More precisely dated, however, are the large, circular, decorated body shields shown in the kiva murals at Pottery Mound (Hibben 1975), which site was abandoned ca. A.D. 1450-1475. Other, less precisely dated, Pueblo IV murals showing shields are at Awatovi (Smith 1952) and possibly at Pueblo del Encierro (Schaafsma 1965). Aside from murals, Pueblo del Encierro (LA 70) also produced fragments from an actual, possible decorated bison-hide shield: located in a great kiva. This site appears to date between A.D. 1400 and 1520 on the basis of tree-rings (Snow 1976:D-24, D-25, A-138 to A-146).

While the materials of the illustrated shields cannot be directly determined, their shape and size relative to human figures holding them are like the bison-hide shields described in historical records a century later (see above). I therefore suggest that these Pueblo IV depictions are indeed of bison-hide shields, and that the Pottery Mound evidence dates the introduction of this shield technology into the Southwest to the early A.D. 1400s. As with the sinew-backed bow and the mountain lion-skin quiver, the synchronicity of Apachean arrival and the introduction of the new technology is the basis for identifying the Apacheans as the agents of introduction.

13

Hibben suggests "Mexican influence" in the shield designs shown at Pottery Mound, which is in line with his interpretive stance towards Pottery Mound as a whole (1975:4-11, 65, 130). While not denying the existence of Mesoamerican influence in the Southwest at various times and places, I wish to point out that the technology of the bison-hide shield has no apparent equivalent in Mesoamerica. Nuttall's description of Mesoamerican shield construction includes shields of solid wood, of wickerwork and cotton, and a flexible leather or cloth shield that could be rolled up (1892:35). None of these resemble at all the rigid bison-hide shield, thus there is no clear technological link. Hibben, however, has stressed design similarities, which do exist, but prehistoric shield designs from the Northern Plains have as strong and in some cases much stronger resemblances to the designs found on Southwestern shields. This point will be developed further during discussion of the four-pointed star motif (below).

5

THE FOUR-POINTED STAR MOTIF

The four-pointed star motif is closely associated with the bison-hide shield, since it appears as a design painted on such shields by both Apacheans and Pueblo Indians (see Figure 5; also see Wright 1976:19, 50, 64; Hall 1926:Figure 10). By "four-pointed star" I mean literally a sharp-pointed, four-armed figure such as the forms shown in Figure 6. I do *not* extend the term "four-pointed star" to refer to any other four-armed figures, such as crosses (simple or fancy) or the rock art motif known a the "outlined cross".

There are, of course, some individual figures, especially in rock art, where the "sharp-pointed" criterion is not clearly met, or thinness of the arms renders it equivocal whether a particular figure should be classed as a cross or four-pointed star. This problem arises in part due to differences in detail rendered by different rock art recorders. For example, the renditions of a vertical row of four-pointed stars from the Black Hills of South Dakota by Renaud (1936:Plate 2) and Sundstrom (1984:88). But I have attempted to be as consistent as possible when accepting individual figures as examples of four-pointed stars.

Ethnographic data on the Pueblo Indians indicate that the four-pointed star motif is used to represent the morning and evening stars, i.e., to represent planets, while the true stars are represented by small dots or crosses (see discussion in Baldwin 1992). Although there are occasional deviations from this, such as the representation of the true stars of certain important constellations by the four-pointed star motif among the Hopi (see Brody 1991:151), the vast majority of informant-identified uses of the four-pointed star motif conform to this generalization. Among the Pueblo Indians there is a strong association of Morning Star, as a supernatural figure, with warfare and hunting (Baldwin 1992), which explains the use of the four-pointed star motif on shields.

Among modern Apacheans there seems to be no clear distinction between the true stars and the planets. The Navajo mainly use dots or crosses to represent stars, but large bright stars and planets may be represented by diamond shapes or, less frequently, by four-pointed stars (Haile 1947:37, 41). Note that the diamond shape is probably a geometrically simplified version of the four-pointed star.

15

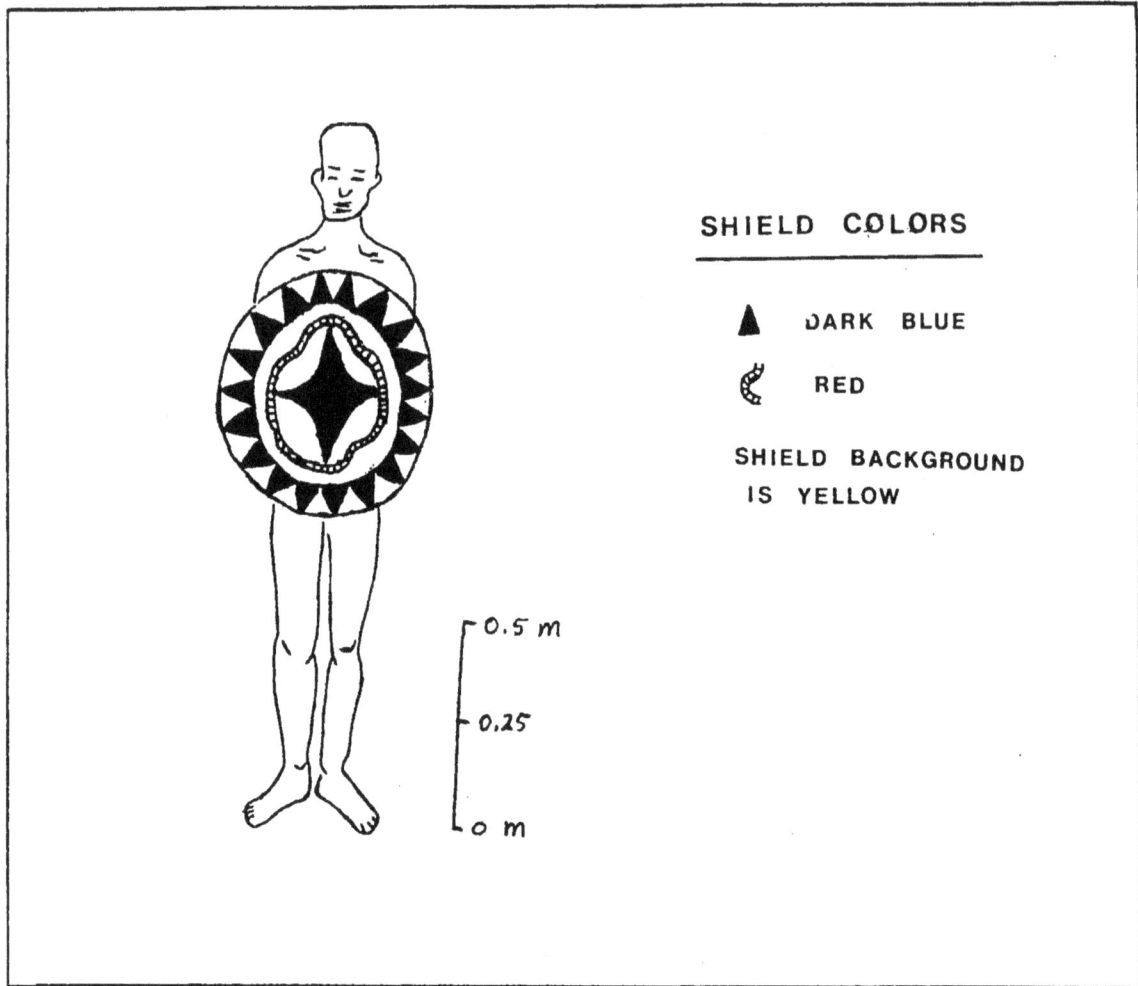

Figure 5. Lipan Apache shield design featuring dark blue four-pointed star. Based on painting by Claudio Linati (1956).

The four-pointed star motif, named *suus* 'star', is used by the Mescalero Apaches, and its meaning is clearly explained by Farrer and Second (see Farrer and Second 1981; Farrer 1991). They demonstrate that the four-pointed star is a visual metaphor for the universe and its creation. Thus, the motif can be used to tap into the fundamental sources of spiritual power for the benefit of human beings. It is used in this way as one of the designs painted on the chests and backs of *gaan* (Mountain Spirit) dancers (Farrer and Second 1981). The use of this motif on Mescalero baskets is discussed in detail by Farrer (1991:77-81, 96-97), and it is found on clothing and in beadwork.

16

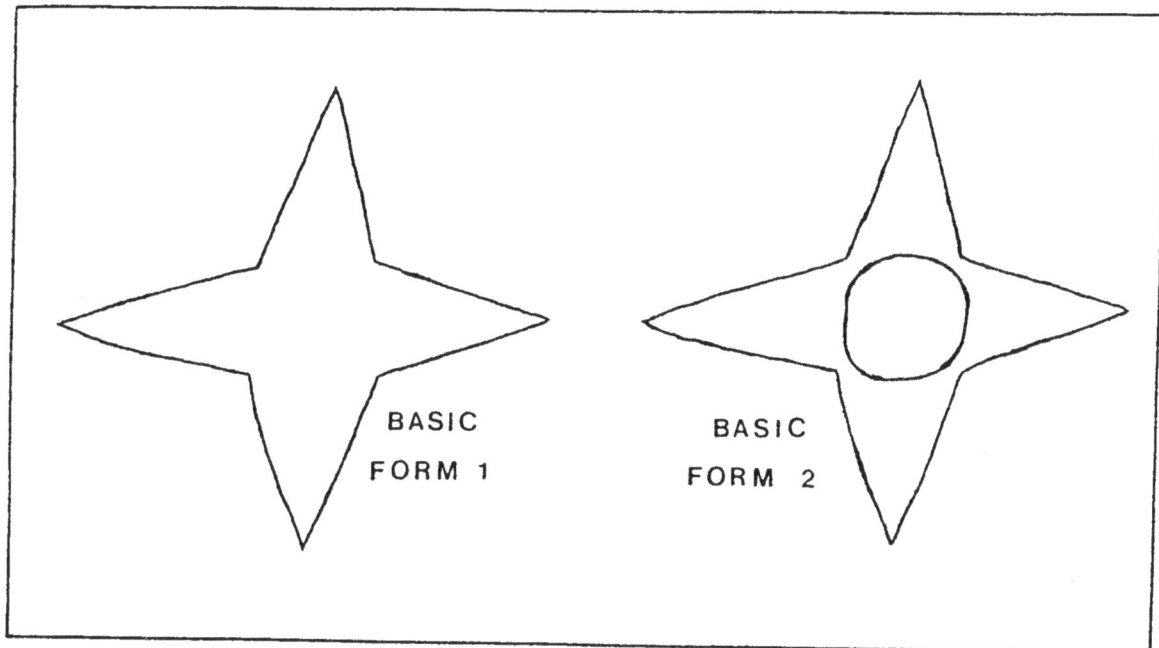

Figure 6. Basic forms of the four-pointed star motif as found in the Southwest culture area. Basic form 1 may appear in solid or outline variations; basic form 2 may appear in solid, outline, or mixed solid/outline variations.

Presumably other Apache groups utilized this motif in the same ways. It is known to have appeared on Apache bison-hide shields, as shown in Linati (1956)(see Figure 5) and Hall (1926:51), and to be used by Chiricahua Apaches on their *gaan* dancers and on the clothing worn by girls during their puberty ceremonies (Opler 1941:83, 109, Plate IV). It seems, then, that Apachean use of the four-pointed star motif is more as a power symbol than as a referent to a particular natural or supernatural celestial entity.

A third Southwestern ethnic group is known to have used the four-pointed star motif: the Tarahumara. Lumholtz (1902:252) illustrates two Tarahumara pottery vessels that he acquired at Panalachic, Chihuahua in 1892, which are decorated with four-pointed stars. The arms of the stars are solid red paint surrounding an unpainted center circle, identical to Basic Form 2 shown in Figure 6. Lumholtz does not discuss this motif, and I have found no further record of it among the Tarahumara.

SOUTHWESTERN ARCHAEOLOGICAL EVIDENCE

I have searched the literature on rock art and decorated pottery of the Southwest prior to A.D. 1300 and have found a complete lack of the four-pointed star motif, with two exceptions. These exceptions are (1) the appearance of a few four-pointed star designs on Mimbres bowls, dating to ca. A.D. 1000-1150 (see Brody *et al.* 1983:58, 103); and (2) a single occurrence of a four-pointed star design on a Sacaton Red-on-buff platter from a Hohokam cremation at Gila Bend, dating to ca. A.D. 900-1150 (Wasley and Johnson 1965:98-99). My suspicion is that these four-pointed star forms resulted through the manipulation of geometric shapes by the painters of the pottery: specifically that they were built up by a juxtaposition of four triangles and thus do not represent a single, discrete symbol (see discussion in Brody *et al.* 1983:110-114). The lack of any further use of the four-pointed star form between A.D. 1150 and 1400 supports the conclusion that there is no significant relationship between the Mimbres and Hohokam use of the form and its post-A.D. 1400 manifestation in the Southwest.

In Pueblo IV there is a sudden blossoming of the use of the four-pointed star motif among the Pueblo Indians, with an apparent close link to the supernatural Morning Star, and thus to the activities of hunting and warfare (see Baldwin 1992, Schaafsma 1992a). The best dated occurrences of the motif are in the kiva murals at Pottery Mound (Hibben 1975:43, 48, 133-135), which probably date between A.D. 1400 and 1450. The motif as shown at Pottery Mound is always a variation of Basic Form 2 (Figure 6), with either a plain center circle or one that has facial features (eyes, nose, and mouth).

Aside from Pottery Mound, the motif occurs widely throughout the area of Pueblo Indian occupation during Pueblo IV, i.e., as far west as Awatovi in Arizona (Smith 1952), but the greatest concentrations of depictions are in the rock art of the Galisteo Basin and Abo Pass (Figure 7). It is notable that the latter two areas are on the frontier with the Southern Plains. And, both kiva murals and rock art show the four-pointed star motif as a shield design. These indications, together with the dating from Pottery Mound, suggest an introduction from the Apacheans ca. A.D. 1400.

SOUTHERN PLAINS DISTRIBUTION OF THE MOTIF

Rock art use of the four-pointed star motif in the Southern Plains seems to coincide with areas that were at one time under the control of Apachean groups (see Figure 7). The three northern sites - an incised outline Basic Form 1 example at Clay Creek, southeastern Colorado (Renaud 1936:Plate 11), a pecked outline Basic Form 1 example at Olive Buttes, east-central New Mexico (Schaafsma 1972:193), and the incised outline of a shield with a Basic Form 2

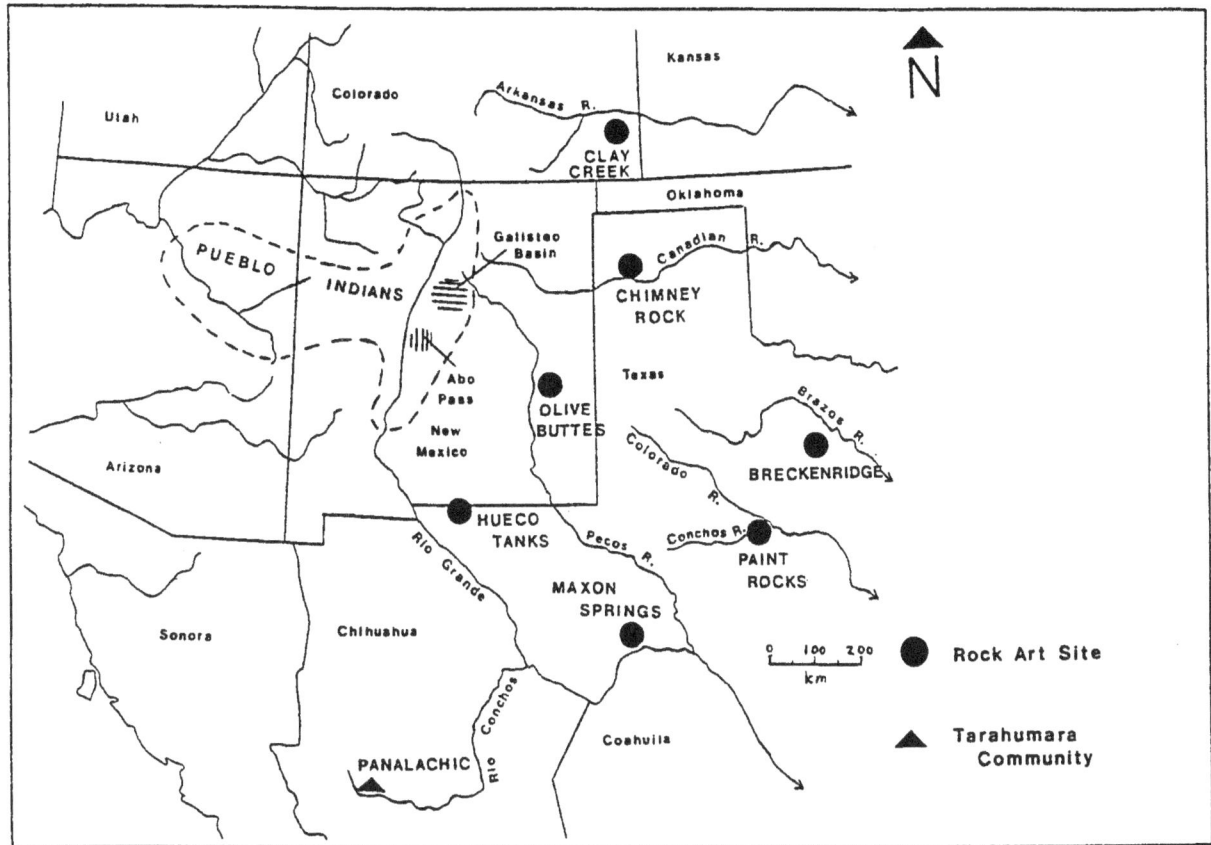

Figure 7. Map showing distribution of the four-pointed star motif in the Southwest and on the southern Plains. Found generally within the Pueblo Indian area after A.D. 1400, with concentrations of rock art occurrences in the Abo Pass and Galisteo Basin. Southern Plains occurrences shown as large dots. Tarahumara occurrence shown as a triangle.

motif near Chimney Rock on the Canadian River in the Texas panhandle (Newcomb and Kirkland 1967:214) - are also probably the oldest, being in territory occupied by Apacheans before A.D. 1700.

The four other sites in Texas all probably post-date A.D. 1700, when the surrounding territories were utilized by Lipan and Mescalero Apaches, and they are all pictographs (Davis and Toness 1974:41, 64; Lowrance 1986:24; Jackson 1938:269, 273, 434; Newcomb and Kirkland 1967:149, 154, 170, 183, 191). The examples at the Hueco Tanks Site may not be Apache in origin, since they could have been made by Pueblo Indians who were settled at El

Paso in A.D. 1680. The mask with the two green four-pointed stars as eyes is the one most likely of Pueblo Indian origin (Davis and Toness 1974:64).

OTHER ETHNOGRAPHIC AND ARCHAEOLOGICAL EVIDENCE

Hibben (1975:30, 134) suggests Mesoamerican connections for shield designs shown in the Pottery Mound murals. The four-pointed star motif is not among the shield designs illustrated by Nuttall (1892), and I am not aware of any use of this motif in Mesoamerica. However, the four-pointed star does appear in scattered rock art and ethnographic use on the Great Plains.

My research on Great Plains ethnographic use of the four-pointed star motif is incomplete at this point, but the motif is known to appear on Cheyenne, Arapaho and Dakota shields and shield covers, and in other limited usage among the Kiowa, Omaha and Ponca. Its significance is variable, ranging from representing the morning star among the Arapaho (Kroeber 1902:135), or a shooting star among the Kiowa (Mooney 1898:260-261), to being a symbol of night among the Omaha and Ponca (Fletcher and La Flesche 1911:504-507). It is extensively used by the Pawnee as a general symbol for both true stars and planets (Chamberlain 1982), and appears to have similar use by the Dakota (Wissler 1907:34-35).

Archaeological evidence from four sites indicates the prehistoric use of the four-pointed star motif in the Northern Plains (see Figure 8). The Kobold Site in southern Montana has among its petroglyphs two incised shields with four-pointed star motifs (Frison 1970:26, 31). The first is a shield-bearing warrior whose shield carries an outline Basic Form 2 motif, while the second is a shield with a variation of Basic Form 2 (Figure 9). Another shield-bearing warrior is found at the Langstaff Site in southern Montana (Lewis 1985:237-238; 1990:78-79). This black paint pictograph shows an outline Basic Form 1 motif on the shield (Figure 9).

In this same area of Montana, Loendorf (1988, 1990) has recently radiocarbon dated a pictographic shield and shield-bearing warrior rock art panel (24-CB-1094) to between A.D. 1035 and 1174. A significant technical detail of the dated panel is that the rock surface had been smoothed before application of the paint. This same preparation of the rock surface is seen at the Langstaff Site (Lewis 1985:237). A stylistic detail linking 24-CB-1094 and the Langstaff Site is that at the former one of the shield-bearing warriors has a right leg ending in a foot turned to the side but a left leg ending in a point (see Loendorf 1990:48). The shield-bearing warrior with the four-pointed star motif at Langstaff has the same stylistic treatment of his two legs (see Lewis 1990:79). These two details suggest the strong possibility that the two sites were created by the same ethnic group, and thus that the dating range for 24-CB-1094 may apply generally to Langstaff. It is not clear from Frison's description whether or not the Kobold Site

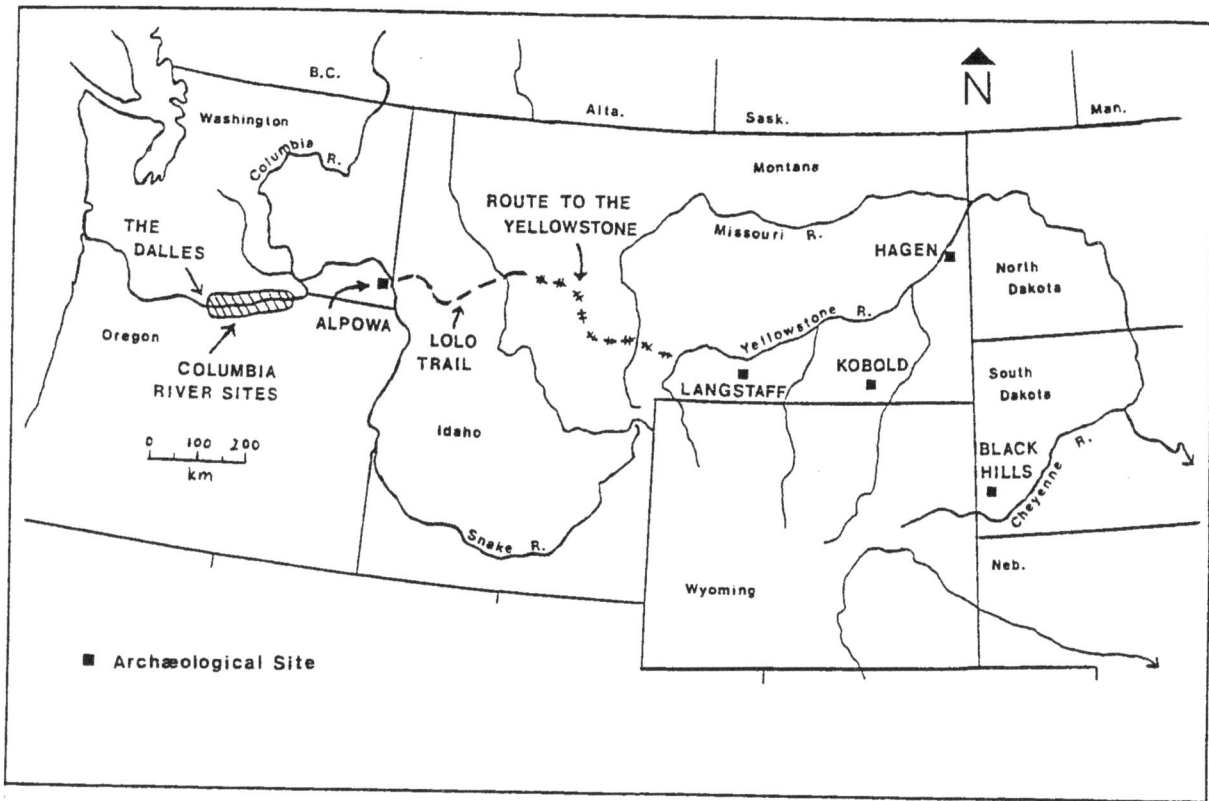

Figure 8. Map showing distribution of the four-pointed star motif at archaeological sites in the Northern Plains and along the Columbia River. Also shown is the possible trade route along the Lolo Trail and through western Montana.

petroglyphs are on a prepared rock surface like those at Langstaff and 24-CB-1094, but the four-pointed star motif suggests a connection to Langstaff, at least.

Based on the radiocarbon dating for 24-CB-1094, Loendorf (1990:51-52) has questioned Keyser's (1975) attribution of the appearance of shield-warrior and shield motifs in Northern Plains rock art to the arrival of Shoshonean-speaking peoples from the Great Basin. Keyser's attribution has also been criticized elsewhere for other reasons (see discussion in Magne and Klassen 1991:415-416). An alternative ethnic attribution for the rock art at 24-CB-1094 mentioned by Loendorf is a possible association with Athapaskan-speakers (Apacheans). Presumably, this tentative ethnic attribution can be expanded to include the other rock art sites in Montana and Wyoming that Loendorf (1990:50) sees as having characteristics similar to 24-CB-1094, such as the Castle Garden Site in central Wyoming.

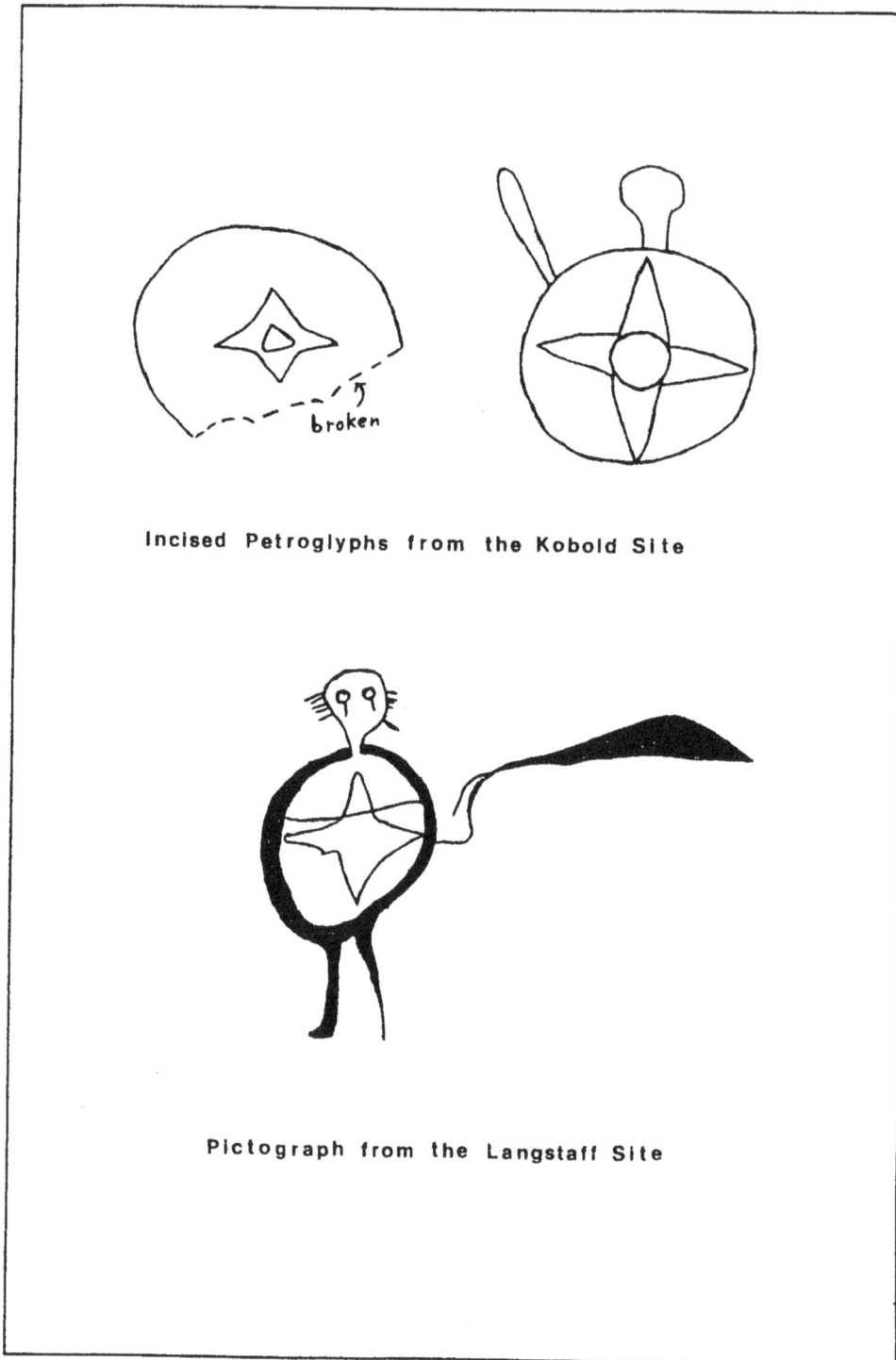

Incised Petroglyphs from the Kobold Site

Pictograph from the Langstaff Site

Figure 9. Petroglyph and pictograph shields with four-pointed star motif from southern Montana.

Taken as a whole, Loendorf's complex of rock art sites displays the following characteristics: (a) the frequent preparation of the rock face by smoothing, (b) the high frequency of shields and shield-bearer motifs, (c) the frequent co-occurrence of incising and painting on individual figures, and (d) the use of the color green. Loendorf *does* suggest that this combination of elements may be indicative of work by a single cultural group.

At this point I wish to point out that this combination of elements is also found in early Navajo rock art of the *Dinetááh* in northwestern New Mexico (Schaafsma 1980:306-312). Another element connecting early Navajo rock art of the *Dinetááh* with Northern Plains rock art is the presence of V-necked, rectangular-bodied anthropomorphs in both areas (Schaafsma 1980:Figure 257; Magne and Klassen 1991). These points lend weight to the possibility that the Montana and Wyoming sites were produced by Apacheans before their arrival in the Southwest.

A vertical set of eight red four-pointed stars, with central circles and thin rays, is present at a rock art site in the southern Black Hills of South Dakota (Sundstrom 1984:88). Sundstrom (1984:111-112) points out their similarity to star designs made by the Dakota, but they also resemble the thin-rayed stars used by the Pawnee. Either ethnic attribution seems reasonable as they do not seem to fit stylistically with the other rock art four-pointed stars noted immediately above.

The final Northern Plains archaeological example of the four-pointed star motif is found incised three times into an antler "bracelet" found at the Hagen Site, eastern Montana (Mulloy 1942:74-75). To me, at least, this "bracelet" looks like a bowguard, thus hinting at a hunting and/or warfare association for the artifact. The form of this four-pointed star is a variation on Basic Form 2 (Figure 10).

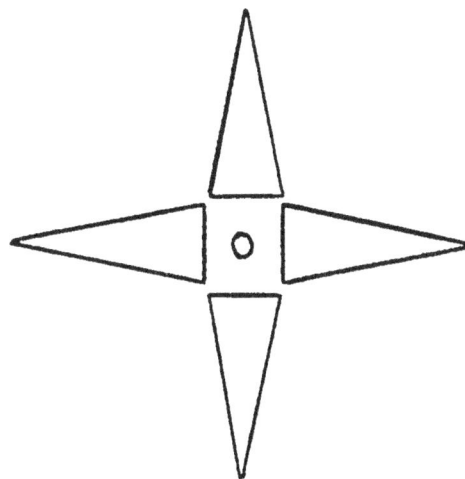

Figure 10. Incised design on "bracelet" from the Hagen Site in eastern Montana.

The Hagen Site has usually been interpreted as an early Crow village that should date to ca. A.D. 1675-1700 (Wood and Downer 1977:85-88). However, the three corrected radiocarbon dates from the Hagen Site - two of A.D. 1169 ± 135 and one of A.D. 1434 ± 137 (Davis 1982:7) - fail to conform to the expected date which is based on artifact typology, hence are rejected by Wood and Downer. It occurs to me, however, that the Hagen Site may have seen *several* temporally discrete occupations, hence the radiocarbon dates may be valid expressions of two of them. The possibility thus exists that the antler "bracelet" may date to the relatively early period of A.D. 1034-1304 given by two of the radiocarbon dates. Note that this range overlaps the A.D. 1035-1174 range for Loendorf's rock art panel.

Tentatively then, the four-pointed star motif may be traced back in time and space to the A.D. 1000s and 1100s in southern Montana and northern Wyoming, with the Apacheans - before their move south - as the possible users.

COLUMBIA RIVER OCCURRENCES

There is another area of prehistoric western North America where the four-pointed star appears in rock art: at over a dozen rock art sites on both sides of the lower Columbia River in Washington and Oregon from the vicinity of The Dalles eastward for about 90 km (Loring and Loring 1982:35-201). Figure 11 illustrates the two most common forms of these four-pointed stars, but there is considerable individual variation. The four-pointed stars may be incised, pecked, or painted in red, or red and white paint, and there is an example combining pecking and red paint at one site (Loring and Loring 1982:198). Many of the rock art sites have more than one example of the four-pointed star.

Except for a single example of this motif at the Alpowa Site on the west bank of the Snake River in extreme eastern Washington (Loring and Loring 1982:136), the series of sites along the lower Columbia River are the only appearances of the four-pointed star motif in Oregon or Washington. This very restricted geographic distribution leads me to suspect that they are connected to the aboriginal trading center associated with The Dalles, a group of rapids breaking the flow of the river. A datum supporting this idea is that many (if not all) of the rock art sites containing the four-pointed star motif are closely associated with prehistoric campsites.

The Dalles area is well-known as an important trading center during historic times, acting as a meeting place for traders from the Northwest Coast on the west, the Columbia Basin on the north and east, and the Great Basin on the south (Griswold 1970:19-20). Historically, it is known that Great Plains goods were brought to The Dalles by groups such as the Nez Perce. It is reasonable to expect that The Dalles functioned as a major trading center in prehistoric times, as well as historically.

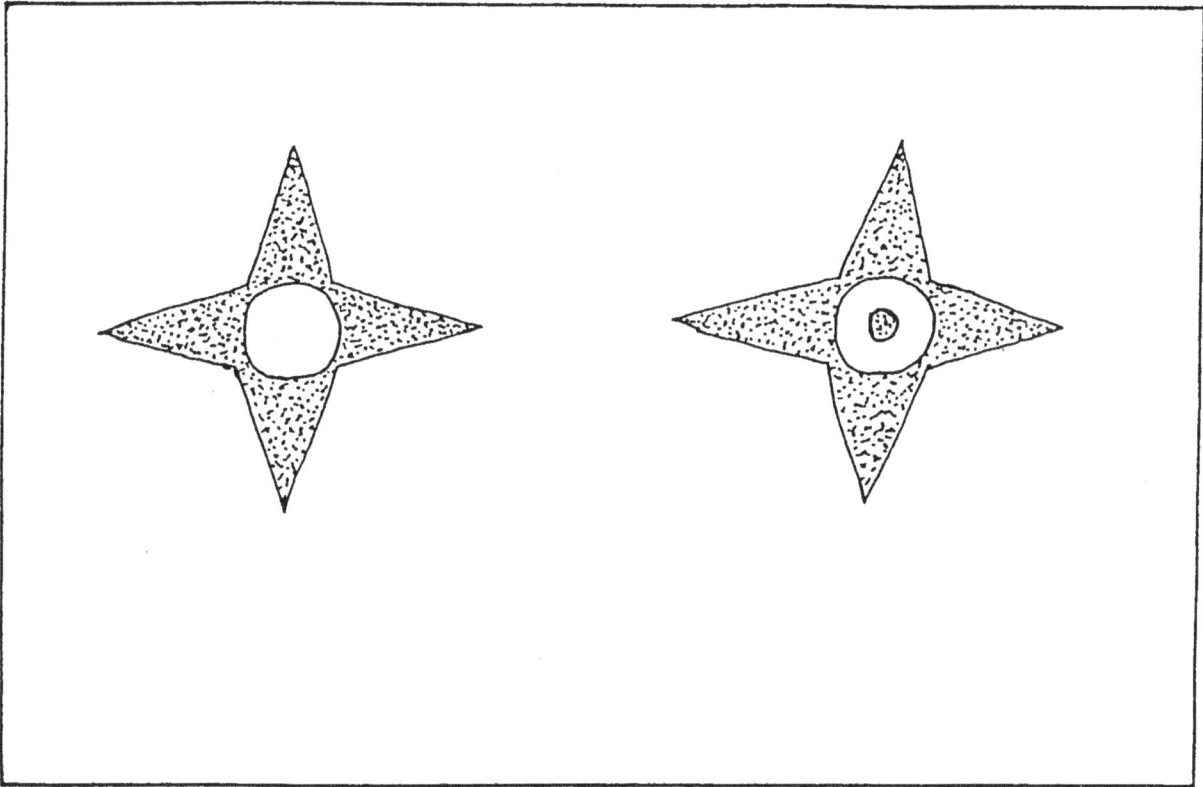

Figure 11. Basic variations on the four-pointed star motif found at Columbia River rock art sites. Red paint may substitute for pecked areas shown.

I therefore offer the suggestion that, concurrent with their postulated occupation of the southern Montana/northern Wyoming area ca. A.D.1000-1200, the Apacheans were in the habit of travelling west to trade at The Dalles. Local goods such as bison products and obsidian from the Yellowstone sources could have been their trade goods. Their trading parties might have camped at various places along the Columbia River upstream from The Dalles, and while at these spots pecked, incised or painted the four-pointed star power symbol onto nearby rocks as a protective device to help guard them from misfortune while in strange territory.

The Alpowa Site occurrence of the motif supports this speculation as it is associated with a convenient camping spot on the route between The Dalles and southern Montana. Note that the Alpowa Site is near the western end of a major aboriginal trail, the Lolo Trail, that crosses the Rocky Mountains from Montana (Griswold 1970:23; McLeod 1980) and is a likely and direct route for the Apacheans to take (see Figure 8).

SUMMARY

The evidences presented above suggest that the four-pointed star motif was used by the Apacheans at a time, ca. A.D.1000-1200, when they occupied an area of southern Montana/northern Wyoming. The Apacheans' use of the motif was on two levels: (1) a primary, abstract level as a power symbol, and (2) a secondary, concrete level as a star symbol. This latter usage they shared with other Great Plains groups, such as the Pawnee.

When the Apacheans moved south to the Southern Plains and the Southwest, they brought the four-pointed star motif with them. There it was adopted by the Pueblo Indian groups as a power symbol strongly linked to the Morning Star supernatural. It may also have been acquired from the Apaches by some Tarahumara after they reached Chihuahua.

6

THE HEARTLINE MOTIF

Despite being generally well-known to anthropologists working in the Southwest and Great Plains, there is surprisingly little analysis and discussion of the heartline motif in the literature. The motif itself is known by several different terms: heartline, lifeline, lifeline heart, line of life, and breathline.

The two basic elements of the motif are (1) a line, usually beginning at or near the mouth of an animal or the head of an anthropomorph, that runs into the body, where it joins with (2) the "heart", a triangular, diamond-shaped, bullet-shaped, oval, or circular element. Sometimes present is a third element: what I will call the "collar", a line at or below the neck that may cross the line of the heartline at right angles (Figure 12), or may form a V-shape from the tip of which the heartline begins (Figure 21).

The first element, the line, is generally assumed to represent the mouth and trachea/esophagus, while the second is called the "heart". This may be misleading, since the second element may have represented more than just the heart to the users of the motif. For example, there is a Navajo collective term *'ajei* for the thoracic organs: the lungs, liver and heart (Young and Morgan 1980). While not generally known, there is an equivalent term in English: the pluck "a butcher's term for the heart, liver, and lights [lungs] of an animal" (Skeat 1909:459). Thus, the second element may be better understood in terms of aboriginal butchering practices than in terms of modern analytical anatomy.

Then again, in some contexts the heartline motif may represent more spiritual aspects, such as the "soul" or "spirit" of the being depicted, rather than any set of physical organs. For example, the motif is known to the Zunis as the *oneyalh kwatona*, the "sacred entrance road" of the Breath of Life (soul). The term as given in Cushing (1886:515) I have slightly rewritten and retranslated through reference to Newman's dictionary (1958:15, 36).

27

THE HEARTLINE IN THE SOUTHWEST

There is no evidence of the heartline motif in the Southwest culture area before A.D. 1300. Known distribution of the heartline motif after A.D. 1400 is shown in Figure 13. The earliest datable use of the motif by Pueblo Indians is the wall painting of a black male bison with a red heartline from the ruined pueblo of Kuaua (Dutton 1963:73-75, 79). Unfortunately, this mural is only shown in black-and-white illustrations, in which the red heartline is not visible. Kuaua was probably a Tiwa pueblo and the mural probably dates to the A.D. 1500s.

The next datable appearance of the motif is on a Matsaki Polychrome bowl from the ruined Zuni pueblo of Hawikuh (Figure 12) that has two very clear examples, both of a heartline with a collar element. Matsaki Polychrome is estimated to date from ca. A.D. 1475 to 1680 by Smith *et al.* (1966:326), while Kintigh (1985:15) suggests a span from ca. A.D. 1400 to 1680.

At the Pueblo IV prehistoric ruin of Pueblo del Encierro (LA 70) there are fragmentary wall paintings with circular designs identified as "shields". In at least two cases "each of these shields is flanked by a fragment of an animal with a heart line" (Schaafsma 1965:11). I have examined the published illustrations several times, but have been unable to convince myself that the heartline motif is actually present.

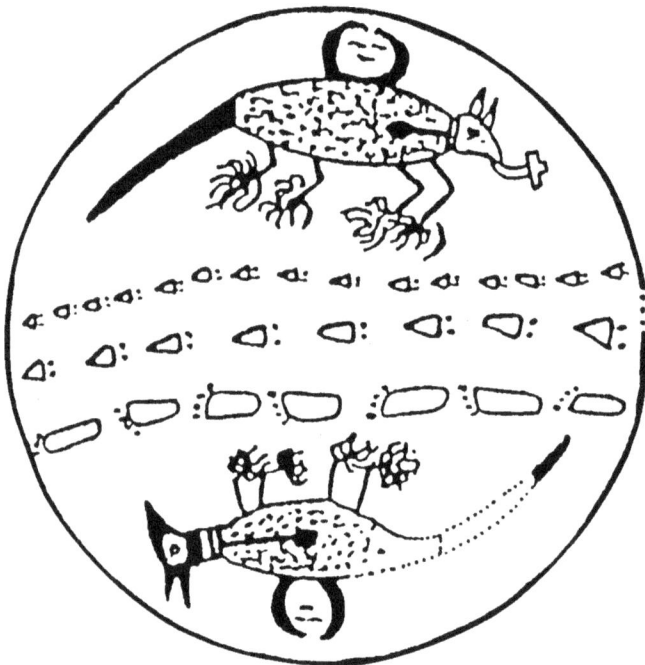

Figure 12. Design on Matsaki Polychrome bowl from Hawikuh, New Mexico, showing the earliest known Zuni example of the heartline motif. From Smith *et al.* (1966:326).

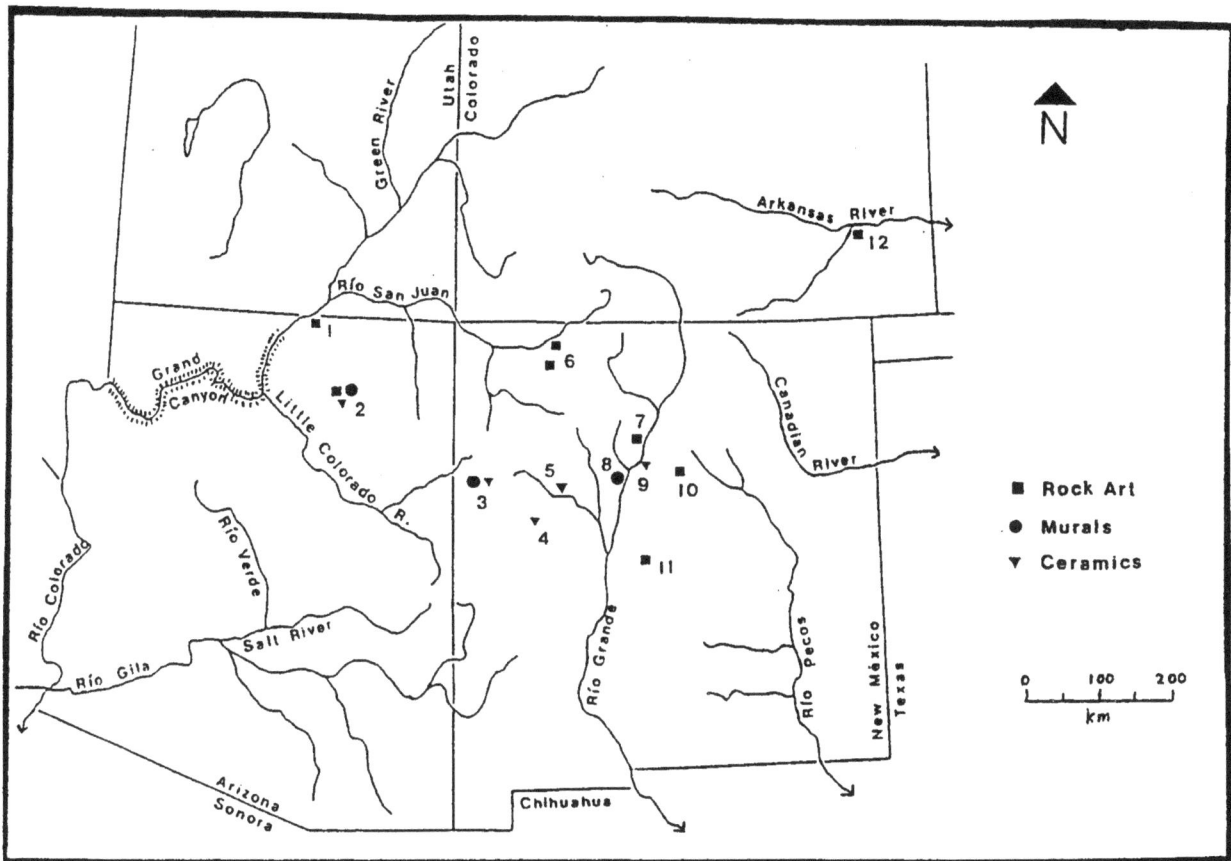

Figure 13. Known distribution of the heartline motif in the Southwest, after A.D. 1400.

KEY:

1 = Glen Canyon, Arizona/Utah border (Turner 1963:48).

2 = Hopi Mesas, Arizona (Turner 1963:48; Bourke 1884:132; Wade & McChesney 1981:234-235)

3 = Zuni, New Mexico (Smith and others 1966:326; Bunzel 1929:94-95; Stevenson 1909:Plate 108; Cushing 1883:Plates 10, 11).

4 = Acoma, New Mexico (Sides 1961:Plate 25b).

5 = Laguna, New Mexico (Stevenson 1883:Figure 591).

6 = *Dinetááh* area, New Mexico (Schaafsma 1963:37, 41-42; 1980:317).

7 = White Rock Canyon, New Mexico (Schaafsma 1975:70-71).

8 = Kuaua Ruin, New Mexico (Dutton 1963:73-75, 79).

9 = Santo Domingo, New Mexico (Chapman 1936:Plate 4a).

10= Galisteo Basin, New Mexico (Sims 1963:216, 218, 220).

11= Abo Pass, New Mexico (herein, and in Baldwin 1986:14).

12= Site C 31, Animas County, Colorado (Renaud 1936:32).

Ethnographic evidence indicates the Zunis as the main users of the heartline motif among the Pueblo Indians. Their term for the motif has been noted above, and the motif seems to be fully integrated with the Zuni concept of the "Breath of Life" (soul) of an animate being. The motif is most familiar from its use as part of a stylized deer design on modern Zuni pottery (see Bunzel 1929:94-95), but is also used with the plumed serpent, the mountain lion, the bear, and others on pottery, wall paintings, and ceremonial paraphernalia (Bunzel 1929:92-93; Stevenson 1909:Plate 108; Cushing 1883:Plates 10 and 11).

The Hopis are also known to use the heartline motif, the earliest ethnographic report in A.D. 1881 being of two pronghorn antelopes with heartlines painted on a kiva wall at Sichomovi (Bourke 1884:132, Plate 25). Watson Smith (1952:96) briefly discusses the possible introduction of the motif to Sichomovi from Zuni, which origin is clarified by the discussion of Zuni-influenced Hopi ceramics by Wade and McChesney (1981:143). Apparently a period of severe drought in the A.D. 1860s forced some Hopis to emigrate to Zuni where they intermarried and were otherwise influenced by their hosts. When they returned to the Hopi Mesas they introduced Zuni designs that are clearly seen on the pottery, including the heartline motif (Wade and McChesney 1981:234, 235).

Turner (1963:48) illustrates three petroglyph bighorn sheep with heartlines in Glen Canyon on the Utah/Arizona border. These are probably attributable to modern Hopi hunting use of the area. Turner also notes very similar petroglyph deer and antelope with heartlines as occurring near Oraibi pueblo.

A few instances of use of the heartline on pottery vessels are known from various pueblos such as Acoma (Sides 1961:Plate 25b), Laguna (Stevenson 1883:Figure 591), Santo Domingo (Chapman 1936:Plate 4a), and San Ildefonso (Chapman 1970:244-245). These all appear to be cases of influence by the Zuni deer-with-heartline design (see discussions by Chapman [1936:38; 1970:244] of Zuni influence). Finally, it is notable that there are *no cases* of the heartline motif being used with an anthropomorphic figure among the Pueblo Indians.

In keeping with the theme of this study, I suggest that the Zunis acquired the heartline motif from the Apacheans, most probably from the Navajos. This has been proposed before by Polly Schaafsma (1963:57):

> It has been suggested (Dittert, 1962, personal communication) that the Athapascans brought the use of the heartline with them into the Southwest as either an Athapascan trait or one which they picked up from Plains groups.

As far as I am aware at present, ethnographers have not recorded the use of the heartline motif among any of the Apache groups. However, among the Navajo there are several uses of the heartline in sandpaintings of the Shooting Chant, where a bighorn sheep, pairs of bison, and mythical animals called "water ox" and "water horse" are shown with definite heartlines (Newcomb and Reichard 1975:62-64, Plates 18, 23-28, 33). In most cases, the heartline is a double line of red and blue reaching from the mouth to the "heart", but in Plate 24 the collar element is present in all of the bison figures. Also note that in Plate 27 each bison "has an arrow or a cane sticking into its heart to show by what means it has been conquered" (Newcomb and Reichard 1975:63).

Earlier examples exist as petroglyphs in the *Dinetááh*, the Navajo traditional homeland in northwestern New Mexico, where 10 bison with heartlines are pecked into a panel at the confluence of the San Juan and Pine Rivers, and a deer or elk with a heartline is pecked into a panel in Largo Canyon (Schaafsma 1963:37, 41-42; 1980:317). Note that the deer/elk and two of the bison are shot through the heart with arrows. These petroglyphs seem reliably attributable to the Navajo and have been dated to the Gobernador Phase, ca. A.D. 1700-1775 (Schaafsma 1963:54), although the possibility of an earlier, Dinetah Phase, date must be considered.

There remain to be considered several petroglyphs that may be of Apachean origin. At LA 10119, a petroglyph site along the Rio Grande in White Rock Canyon, are an outline doe deer and a bird with heartlines (Schaafsma 1975:70-71). In the Galisteo Basin there are a possible deer and a bison with heartlines, plus a mythical creature with a possible heartline variant (Sims 1963:216, 218, 220). And from Abo Pass, central New Mexico, there are three petroglyphs showing heartlines: (1) an outline mountain lion with a bullet-shaped "heart" element (Baldwin 1986:14); (2) two unidentified animals in the same style, the larger of which has a prominent heartline (Figure 14, top); and (3) a bear that is wounded by an arrow (Figure 14, bottom).

After the withdrawal of the Pueblo Indians from Abo Pass ca. A.D. 1675, that area is known to have been occupied by Apaches and various archaeological sites there are assigned to the Apache Horizon, ca. A.D. 1650-1850 (Baldwin 1983). I attribute the Abo Pass heartline examples to these Apaches, including the mountain lion - which I had previously attributed to the Tompiro Pueblo Indians - because it now seems to me to be an Apache attempt to copy the style of older Pueblo Indian petroglyphs, but with the heartline addition.

A common characteristic of the Abo Pass examples is that they are pecked outlines, with only a few solidly pecked elements. This characteristic is shared by the examples cited from White Rock Canyon and the Galisteo Basin, thus giving weight to the suggestion that they also are of Apachean origin.

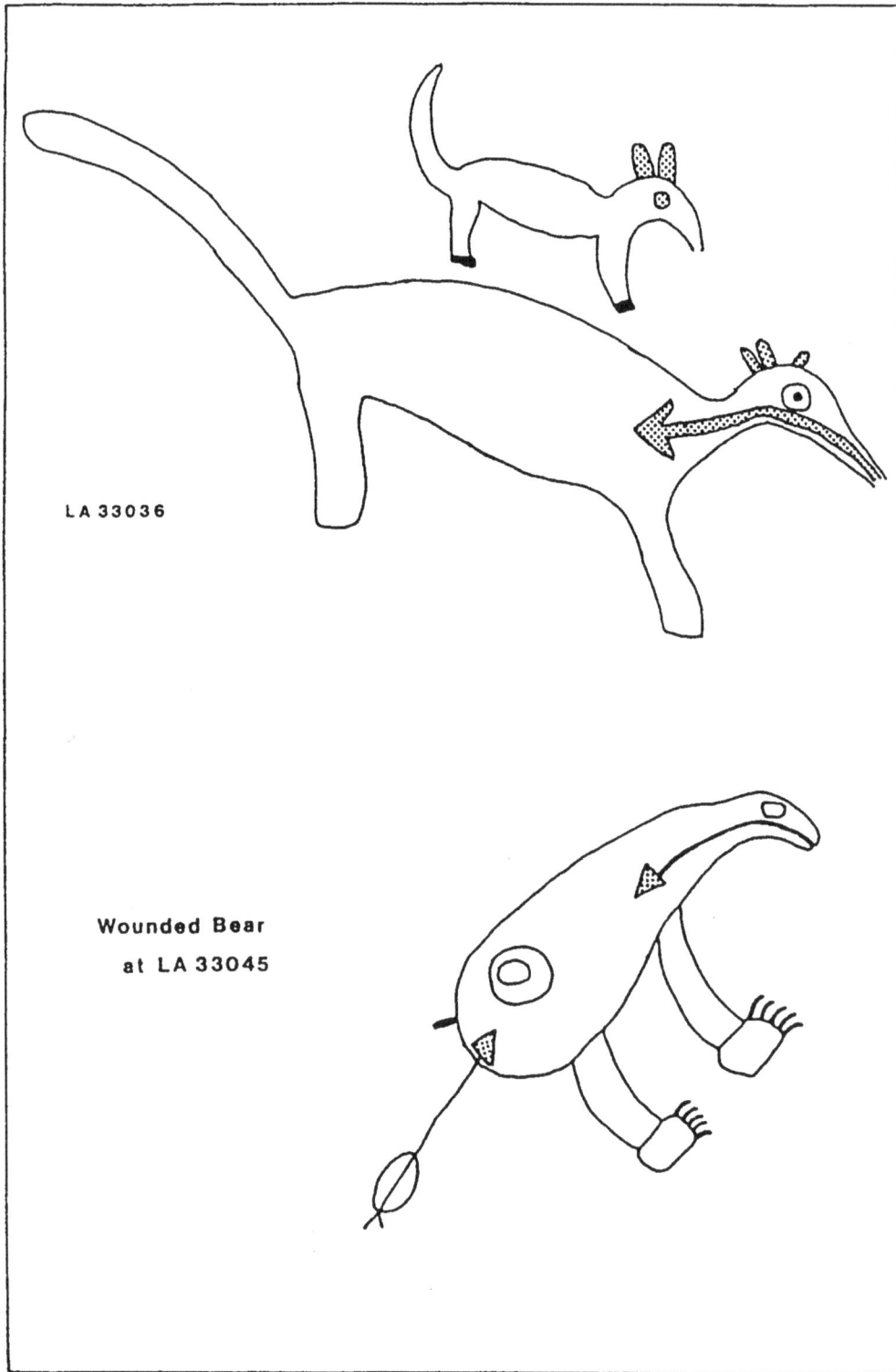

Figure 14. Incised and pecked petroglyphs with heartline motif from two sites at Abo Pass, central New Mexico. Stippled areas are pecked.

LA 33036

Wounded Bear
at LA 33045

Of modern, non-aboriginal origin are the two pictograph panels in the Sierra Blanca Mountains of southeastern New Mexico that include a pronghorn antelope with a heartline (Schaafsma 1992b:157). Finally, in southeastern Colorado - within the earliest historically recorded range of the Apacheans - is a petroglyph site containing an outline bison and another outline animal, both with heartlines (Renaud 1936:32 and Plate 16, Figure 3).

Based upon only Southwestern evidences, it would be easy to argue in favor of a Zuni invention of the heartline motif, rather than for an Apachean origin. An Apachean origin becomes most convincing after consideration of the evidence from the Northern Plains and elsewhere in North America.

THE HEARTLINE IN THE NORTHERN PLAINS, AND BEYOND

Ethnographic evidence of the heartline motif is strongest for the Blackfoot, from the northwestern extreme of the Great Plains, and the Ojibwa from the northeastern Great Plains and adjacent subarctic woodlands. Also known as the Ojibway, Chippewa, Bungi, and Saulteaux, the Ojibwa occupied a large territory stretching from Saskatchewan, Manitoba and North Dakota through northern parts of Minnesota, Wisconsin, Michigan and western Ontario. Hoffman (1891:222) relates that:

> Among the Ojibwa the heartline is used in hunting magic, where a shaman will draw with a sharp-pointed bone or nail, upon a small piece of birch bark, the outline of the animal desired by the supplicant [the hunter]. The place of the heart of the animal is indicated by a puncture upon which a small quantity of vermilion is carefully rubbed, this color being very efficacious toward effecting the capture of the animal and the punctured heart insuring its death. Frequently the heart is indicated by a round or triangular figure, from which a line extends toward the mouth, generally designated the life line, i.e., that magic power may reach its heart and influence the life of the subject designated.

Hoffman also notes that drawings in earth or ashes can be used to the same effect.

Mallery (1893:495-496), drawing upon other sources, confirms and expands upon this to the point where it is clear that any picture or image of an animal or human being with the heart represented upon it can be used to supernaturally influence the subject depicted. Hoffman (1891:295-297) and later sources, such as Dewdney (1975:48, 76, 147, 154), illustrate anthropomorph and animal figures with heartlines on Ojibwa birchbark scrolls without commentary as to the significance of the motif in these contexts.

A different interpretive perspective is provided by Blackfoot usage of the heartline motif within paintings of animals and anthropomorphs on tipi covers. These paintings generally represent elements of a personal vision of the creator of the tipi design. Brasser (1978:12) gives the following description:

> The vision is represented by a picture of the spiritual donors, usually animals....these animal figures are either elongated or repeated, ideally four times, so as to fill the available space. Their spiritual nature is indicated by the representation of the so-called 'life-line', kidneys, and jointmarks, which were believed to be sources of their supernatural powers.

Such designs (see Figure 15) were first described for the Blackfoot by Grinnell (1901:660-668), and the heartline motif noted but not explained.

Despite rather sweeping claims for a general use of the heartline motif throughout North America made by some authors, I have not been able as yet to document other ethnographic use of the motif, except for a single instance of a pair of anthropomorphs with heartlines painted upon a Cree tipi cover (Brasser 1979:36).

Figure 15. Bear with heartline and kidney spots, painted on a Blackfoot cloth tipi cover. Drawn by Ron Beckwith from a photograph taken by John C. Ewers in May 1944 (photograph number NA-3324-2 in the photographic archives of the Glenbow Museum, Calgary, Alberta, Canada).

The above ethnographic evidences provide two interpretive possibilities for the archaeological heartline data examined below: (1) the motif used as part of hunting or war magic with the objective of subduing the animal or person depicted; and (2) the motif used to indicate a spiritual link between the being represented and the creator of the depiction. Underlying both of these is a common theme of supernatural influence between the "artist" and the being depicted.

Archaeological evidences from the northern Great Plains and elsewhere in North America are mapped in Figure 17. A major concentration of rock art depictions exists at Writing-on-Stone Provincial Park, Alberta (1 on Figure 17), where many anthropomorphs and a few animal figures contain heartlines (Keyser 1977:26-27, 65, 72, 79). Keyser (1977:51) has applied the "vision quest" interpretation to the presence of heartlines at these sites. Major aspects of Keyser's analysis have been challenged by a second major study (Magne and Klassen 1991), but both studies date the petroglyphs of Writing-on-Stone as ranging from Late Prehistoric (ca. A.D. 1000/1300 to 1700) to Proto-Historic and Historic. Both studies also tend to attribute most of the heartline motif figures to the Late Prehistoric.

Relevant to the above are two anthropomorphic boulder figures from the Alberta and Saskatchewan plains (A and B on Figure 17). One of these, the Cabri Lake Man of Saskatchewan, is shown in Figure 16. These two boulder figures are stylistically identical to the Writing-on-Stone anthropomorphs, and both have heartlines and kidney marks identical to historic Blackfoot tipi cover paintings. While the boulder figures are not directly datable, it seems likely that they are contemporary with the prehistoric rock art of Writing-on-Stone, and further that both the rock art and the boulder figures may be attributable to the Old Women's Phase (ca. A.D. 800-1750) of the northwestern Great Plains (Vickers 1986:95-102; Meyer 1988), which many archaeologists accept as representing the prehistoric Blackfoot.

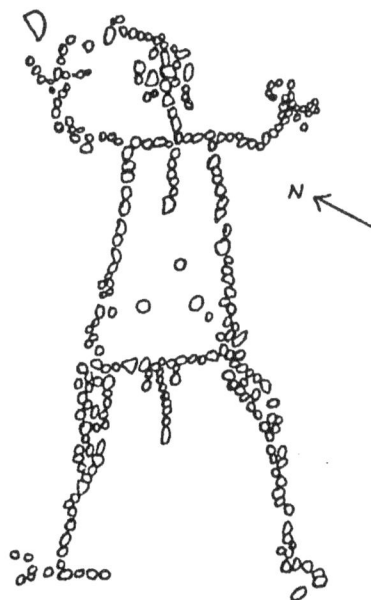

Figure 16. Boulder figure from southwestern Saskatchewan known as the Cabri Lake Man. Based on a photograph by George Tosh. Figure is about 7.5 m tall.

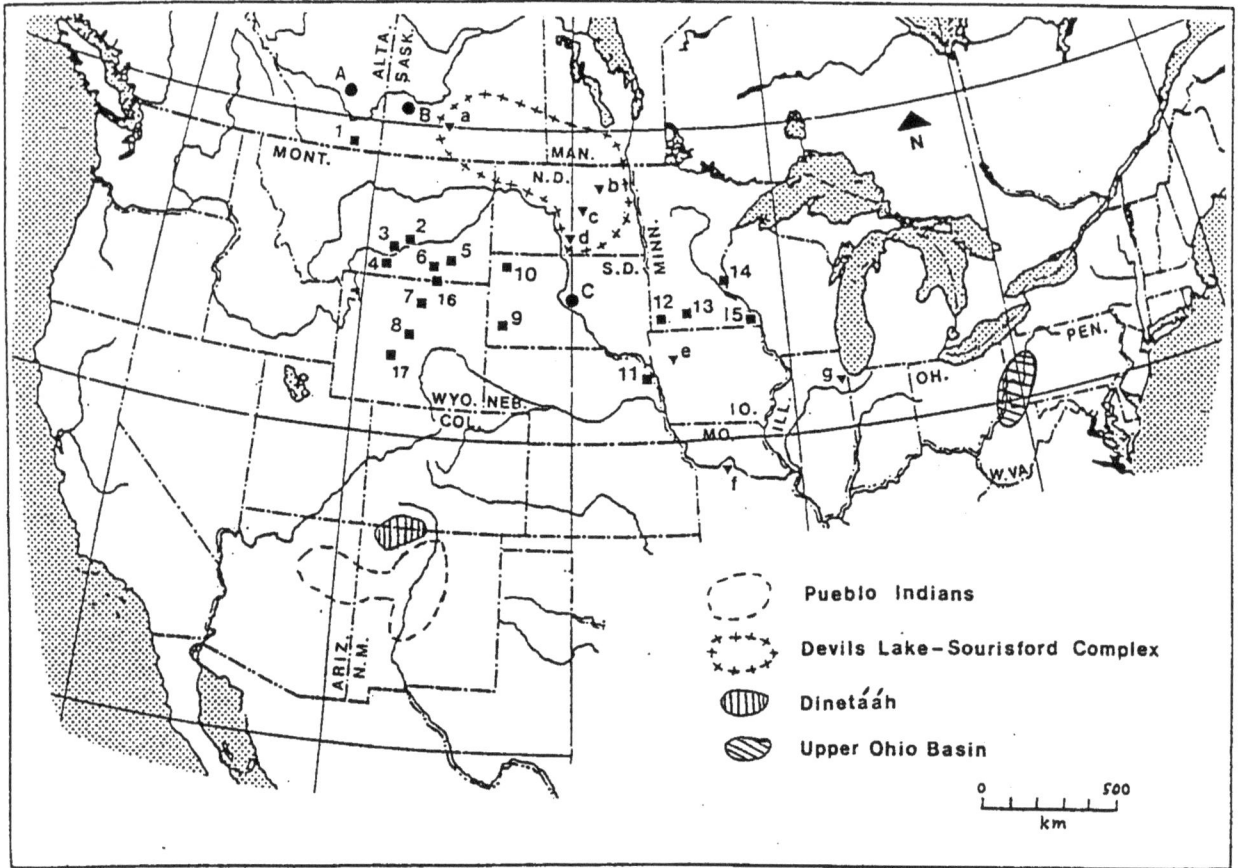

Figure 17. Map of archaeological site locations for heartline motif occurrences in North America. See KEY on facing page.

KEY FOR FIGURE 17:

SQUARES & NUMBERS = ROCK ART

1 = Writing-on-Stone, Alberta (Keyser 1979).
2 = Canyon Creek Site, Montana (Lewis 1985).
3 = Pictograph Cave, Montana (Anonymous 1961:3, 10).
4 = Five Mile Creek Site, Montana (Lewis 1985).
5 = Tipi Rock, Montana (Johnson 1976:42).
6 = Rosebud Medicine Rock, Montana (Badhorse 1979).
7 = Medicine Lodge Creek, Wyoming (Frison 1978:414-415).
8 = Castle Gardens, Wyoming (Renaud 1936:11-13).
9 = Southern Black Hills, South Dakota (Sundstrom 1984:76).
10 = North Cave Hills, South Dakota (Keyser 1984).
11 = Dakota County, Nebraska (Ewers 1982).
12 = Pipestone Quarry, Minnesota (Mallery 1893:87-90).
13 = Jeffers Petroglyphs, Minnesota (Lothson 1976).
14 = Dayton's Bluff Cave & Harvey Rock Shelter, Minnesota (Lothson 1976).
15 = Reno Cave & La Moille Cave, Minnesota (Lothson 1976).
16 = Decker area, Wyoming/Montana border (Carbone 1972; Anonymous 1961).
17 = North Fork Popo Agie Site, Wyoming (Schuster 1987).

DOTS & CAPITAL LETTERS = BOULDER FIGURES

A = Human figure with heartline in Crawling Valley, Alberta (Bryan 1967:286).
B = "Cabri Lake Man" in Saskatchewan (Epp and Dycke 1983:15).
C = Animal figure with heartline near Pierre, South Dakota (Lewis 1889).

TRIANGLES & SMALL LETTERS = ARTIFACTS

a = Catlinite pendant near Gravelbourg, Saskatchewan (Carlson 1989).
b = Catlinite tablet at Devils Lake, North Dakota (Montgomery 1906:645).
c = Heimdal Mound, North Dakota (Howard 1953).
d = Bentz Gorgets from Long Lake Creek Site, North Dakota (Howard 1953).
e = Bastian Site, Iowa (Bray 1963).
f = Utz Site, Missouri (Bray 1963).
g = Anker Site, Illinois (Bluhm and Liss 1961).

In southern Montana, northern Wyoming, and western South Dakota is a cluster of rock art sites (2 through 10, plus 16 and 17 on Figure 17) providing examples of the heartline motif. Most of the examples are animal figures (see Figure 18) but there are some anthropomorphs, and a deer and three bear examples have one or more arrows shot into their bodies. Some of these are from the same sites and panels already mentioned under the discussion of the four-pointed star motif as possibly being part of a rock art complex dating to ca. A.D. 1000-1200 (above). At least some of the others probably date to the same period. I am aware of several other rock art sites with the heartline motif in Wyoming, but the sources are too vague on the locations of these sites to allow them to be plotted in Figure 17.

Syms (1979) has defined the Devils Lake-Sourisford Burial Complex that covers parts of Saskatchewan, Manitoba and North Dakota (see Figure 17). Burial mounds from this complex (b, c and d on Figure 17) have produced a number of artifacts incised with figures bearing the heartline motif (Figure 19), including a catlinite tablet showing a bison with heartline (Montgomery 1906:645, Plate 32d), a whelk shell gorget showing a bear with heartline and an elk antler "collar" with a pair of bison with heartlines (Howard 1953:133). Speculatively, I have added into this complex an isolated find from southwestern Saskatchewan: a catlinite pendant incised with a stylized bear paw that contains a heartline design (Carlson 1989). The complex is dated from ca. A.D. 900 to 1400 and is tentatively identified as the product of people speaking a Siouan language.

Farther to the southeast, in Iowa, Illinois and Missouri, more artifacts incised with the heartline motif have been recovered from archaeological sites (e, f and g on Figure 17). There are two catlinite tablets from the Bastian Site in Iowa, one showing a bison with heartline and an arrow across its body, the other an unidentified animal with heartline that also has an arrow across its body (Bray 1963:20, 26). From central Missouri are four tablets at the Utz Site: two showing bird heads with heartlines, one a thunderbird/man with heartline, and one showing an unidentified animal with heartline (Bray 1963:4-14). Finally, Bluhm and Liss (1961) describe a clay pipe from a burial at the Anker Site near Chicago, Illinois that is incised on each side with a bison containing a large heartline (Figure 20). The arrows across the animals at the Bastian Site call to mind the hunting magic interpretation.

The Bastian, Utz and Anker sites are associated with regional variations of the Oneota Culture, a prehistoric/proto-historic archaeological culture beginning ca. A.D. 1300 and thought to be associated with Siouan-speaking peoples (Fowler and Hall 1978:566). The large Utz Site may have been occupied by ancestors of the Missouri Indians between ca. A.D. 1400 and 1750 (Henning 1970:14-17, 143). The Anker Site of the Huber Phase dates to ca. A.D. 1400-1500 and may represent heavily Oneota-influenced ancestors of the Miami, an Algonquian-speaking people (Bluhm and Liss 1961; Fowler and Hall 1978:566; Brose 1978:581-582).

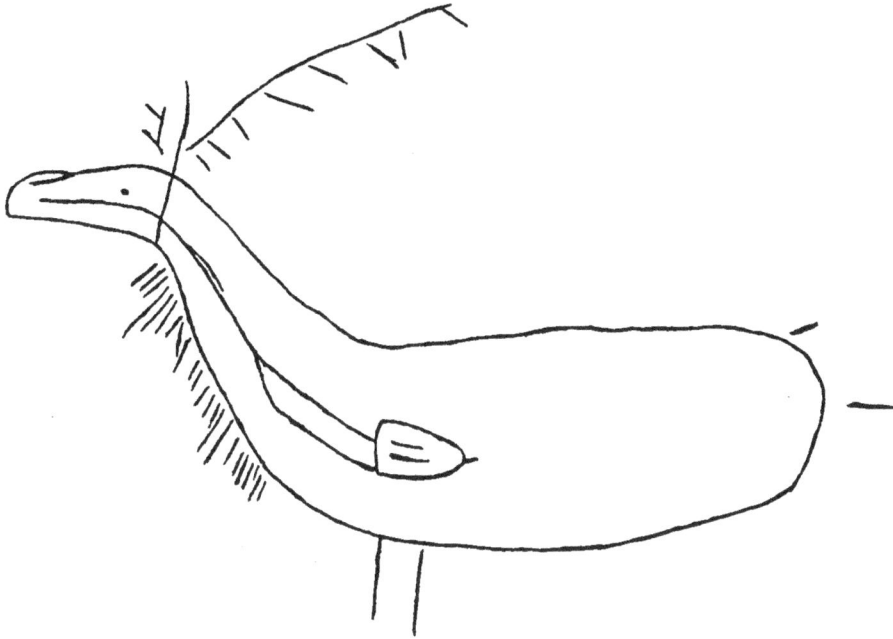

Figure 18. Petroglyph elk with heartline at Rosebud Medicine Rock, southern Montana. Drawing based on photography by Beverly Badhorse (1979). No scale.

Figure 19. Heartline design on incised catlinite tablet from a burial mound at Devils Lake, North Dakota. From Montgomery (1906). No scale.

In southern Minnesota are several rock art sites (12 to 15 on Figure 17) containing petroglyph anthropomorphs, animals and "thunderbirds" with the heartline motif (Lothson 1976). Many of these greatly resemble the incised designs historically used on birchbark scrolls by the Ojibwa, already noted above. However, these petroglyph sites lie south beyond the historical territories or probable prehistoric territories of the Ojibwa. On the other hand, they are within the known range of the Oneota Culture, hence may be associated with Siouan-speaking peoples, as is noted by Lothson (1976:38).

I know of two other examples of the heartline motif along the Missouri River: (1) Mallery (1893:Plate 13) illustrates a panel of petroglyphs from a cliff along the river in Nebraska (11 in Figure 17), that includes a bear with heartline (see also Ewers' [1982:37-38] discussion); and (2) Lewis (1889:162-163) reports a boulder figure of an animal near Pierre, South Dakota (C on Figure 17) that has a heartline with collar (Figure 21).

The final evidences of the heartline motif are found as petroglyphs and pictographs in the Upper Ohio River Basin (see Figure 17). These rock art sites are described and illustrated in Swauger (1974). These mostly depict animals and birds, but there are a few anthropomorphs; about half of those with heartlines also have the collar element. Swauger (1974:108-112) assigns these petroglyphs to the Monongahela Complex, and speculates that these archaeological remains were produced by ancestors of the Shawnee, an Algonquian-speaking people, partly on the basis of the resemblance between the petroglyphs and Ojibwa birchbark scroll figures. Griffin (1978:557-559) dates the Monongahela Complex to A.D. 1000-1600, and notes that while a connection to the historic Shawnee has been sought by archaeologists, it has not yet been demonstrated.

DISCUSSION AND SUMMARY

The most significant archaeological evidence from outside the Southwest appears to be the cluster of rock art sites in southern Montana, northern Wyoming and western South Dakota. These fit in with the rock art sites in this general area already identified as of possible Apachean origin, and tentatively dated to ca. A.D. 1000-1200.

I interpret the other evidences from the northern Great Plains and the American Mid-West as suggesting an origin of the heartline motif somewhere on the northeastern Great Plains periphery sometime before A.D. 900, in what may have been an area of ethno-linguistic mixture of Siouan- and Algonquian-speaking peoples. I suggest that the motif was carried westwards to the Alberta-Montana area by ancestors of the Blackfoot, as represented by the Old Women's Phase after their arrival ca. A.D. 800. During the next four hundred years, ca. A.D. 800-1200, prolonged contact resulted in the transferral of the heartline motif and at least the

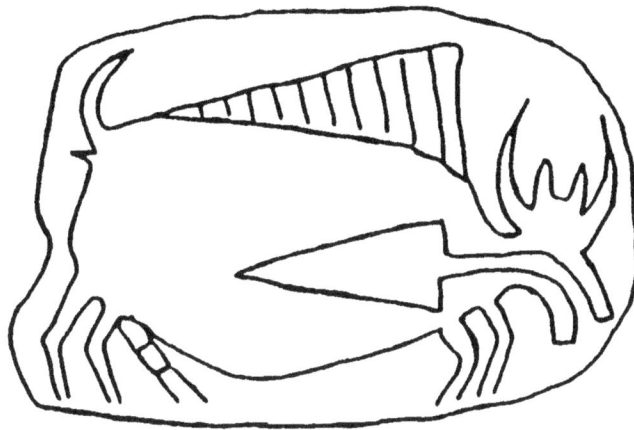

Figure 20. Heartline design incised on clay pipe from the Anker Site, Illinois (Bluhm and Liss 1961). Original is about 10 cm long.

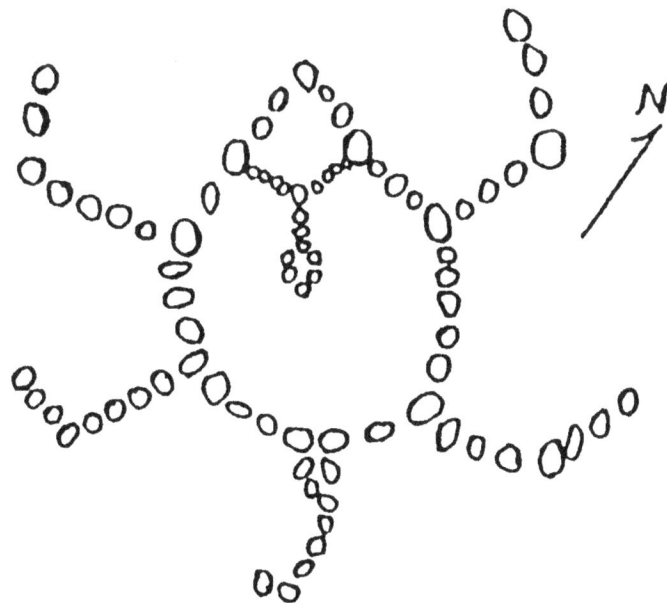

Figure 21. Animal boulder figure with the heartline pendant from V-shaped "collar." Near Pierre, South Dakota (Lewis 1889). Figure is about 5 m wide.

hunting magic significance of it from the Blackfoot ancestors to the Apacheans. This is clearly a speculative scenario, but it seems to fit presently available evidences. It is supported and elaborated upon during discussion of the Apachean migration, below.

Independently of the Apacheans and Blackfoot, the heartline motif seems to have survived in the northeastern Great Plains periphery, perhaps being carried forward in time by the people responsible for the Devils Lake-Sourisford Complex and passed from them to the Oneota Culture, and on to the Ojibwa. How the motif passed eastwards into the Upper Ohio Valley is unclear at present but probably is associated with developments in the prehistory of the Algonquian languages (see Proulx 1980, 1983).

In contrast to the interpretation offered immediately above, Howard (1953:137) includes the heartline motif (or "line of life" as he calls it) among stylistic evidences for influence in the northern Great Plains of the so-called "Southern Cult". I have consulted several publications illustrating "Southern Cult" motifs, including Waring and Holder (1945) and Howard (1968), without finding the inclusion of the heartline motif; note that one of these sources is a later publication by Howard himself. Thus, there seems little support for the idea that the heartline motif originates or comes from somewhere in the southern United States.

In her brief discussion, Habgood (1967:21) notes Eurasian motifs that may be related to the heartline motif of North America. Such wider possible connections are beyond the scope of the present study.

Once brought into the Southwest by the Apacheans, the hunting magic potential of the heartline motif seems to be the conceptual basis for its transmission to the Zunis after A.D. 1400. Its early influence on other Pueblo Indians seems to be transient, the Kuaua example being the only definite case outside of the Zunis before the late A.D. 1800s. The motif's expansion to the Hopis and, sporadically, to some other Pueblo Indians appears to be through the medium of Zuni influence. Its modern survival among Apacheans is only attested for Shooting Chant sandpaintings among the Navajo.

7

ALBERTA TO NEW MEXICO:
A TWO-STAGE APACHEAN MIGRATION

Originally, I had intended to end this study at this point. However, in the course of research on the hunting/warfare complex whose elements are discussed above, certain ideas regarding the Apachean Migration itself have crystallized and I find myself drawn, somewhat reluctantly, into that subject. Consequently, I wish it clearly understood that the following series of ideas on the Apachean migration from Alberta to New Mexico are first approximations and not yet supported through in-depth research.

At the beginning of this study I note that I have always favored an Apachean migration route south from Alberta to New Mexico along the western edge of the Great Plains. This bias, if it be such, guides the discussion below. Recent and current knowledge and interpretations of Great Plains prehistory since ca. A.D. 1 are summarized by various authors in Schlesier (1994), which source should be used for contrast since my tentative interpretations depart, to a greater or lesser degree, from some current viewpoints.

THE APACHEAN EMERGENCE ONTO THE GREAT PLAINS

The Apacheans are presumed to have emerged from the western Boreal Forests (i.e., from the Western Subarctic culture area) somewhere along the ecotone between the forests and the grasslands of the northern Great Plains. This ecotone stretches from central Alberta through central Saskatchewan to southern Manitoba. Following this emergence, it is presumed that the Apacheans then lived upon the northern Great Plains for a period of time before moving south. If this is correct, then presumably the Apacheans might be identifiable with a set of archaeological remains in that region.

Previous suggestions that the Avonlea Phase (ca. A.D. 100-1400) can be equated with the Apacheans are summarized and updated by Haskell (1987) and Wilcox (1988). However, the fundamental basis for an Avonlea/Apacheans equation, that the Avonlea Phase archaeological remains "are in the right places at the right times" (Wilcox 1988:273), is equally applicable to the Besant Phase (ca. 100 B.C. to A.D. 1000). Indeed, a Besant Phase/Apacheans equation is made by Perry (1980:286), which is somewhat incongruous since Perry champions a mountain-based territorial core for the Apacheans but the Besant Phase is clearly plains-based.

The geographic distributions of the Avonlea and Besant phases (shown in Figure 22) are based on those given in Reeves (1983:318-321), but modified with data from other sources (Johnson 1970a, 1970b; Pettipas 1983; Vickers 1986; Morlan 1993, and others). Reeves (1983:10-13) includes the Sonota Complex within Besant, but this is disputed by Syms (1977:91-92), hence in Figure 22 the Sonota Complex is distinguished from Besant.

A curiosity of the Avonlea and Besant phases is that for a considerable period of time (ca. 600 years) these archaeological complexes co-exist in both time and space in southern Alberta, western Saskatchewan, and the Missouri drainage in Montana, as demonstrated in chronological data presented by Morlan (1988:293, 295). Previous interpretations frequently have assumed, either explicitly or implicitly, that the two phases represent two distinct ethno-linguistic groups. This may be called the "co-existing ethnicities" interpretation. The chief weakness of this interpretation is that the two phases are distinguishable with certainty only by the presence of their respective diagnostic projectile points.

I tentatively favor an equation of Besant with the Apacheans, a choice that guides the rest of this discussion. The Besant Phase is characterized by the use of bison jumps and bison pound structures, stone rings that are interpreted as the remains of tipis, and the diagnostic Besant and Samantha projectile points (for details and discussion see Reeves 1983:140-141; Johnson 1970b; Vickers 1986:81-88). The Besant point is presumed to be associated with use of the atlatl, and the Samantha point (appearing ca. A.D. 450) with use of the bow and arrow.

THE FIRST SOUTHWARD WITHDRAWAL

Morlan (1988:304-305) presents a waxing-waning model of Besant/Avonlea chronological relationships: Besant beginning earlier, waxing in frequency, then waning as Avonlea waxes, and disappearing before Avonlea disappears; both phases being replaced by the Old Women's Phase. However, it appears that Morlan's waxing-waning model does not adequately take into account certain geographic relationships. Specifically, Morlan's own chronological charts suggest a progressive geographic replacement of the Besant Phase by the Old Women's Phase (see Figure 23).

Morlan's chronological data indicate that the Old Women's Phase replaces Besant in the Middle Saskatchewan and Assiniboine Basins by ca. A.D. 700, and then proceeds to replace Besant in the Upper Saskatchewan Basin by ca. A.D. 800. The latest Besant Phase dates shown by Morlan all come from the Missouri Basin, where Besant seems to survive until ca. A.D.

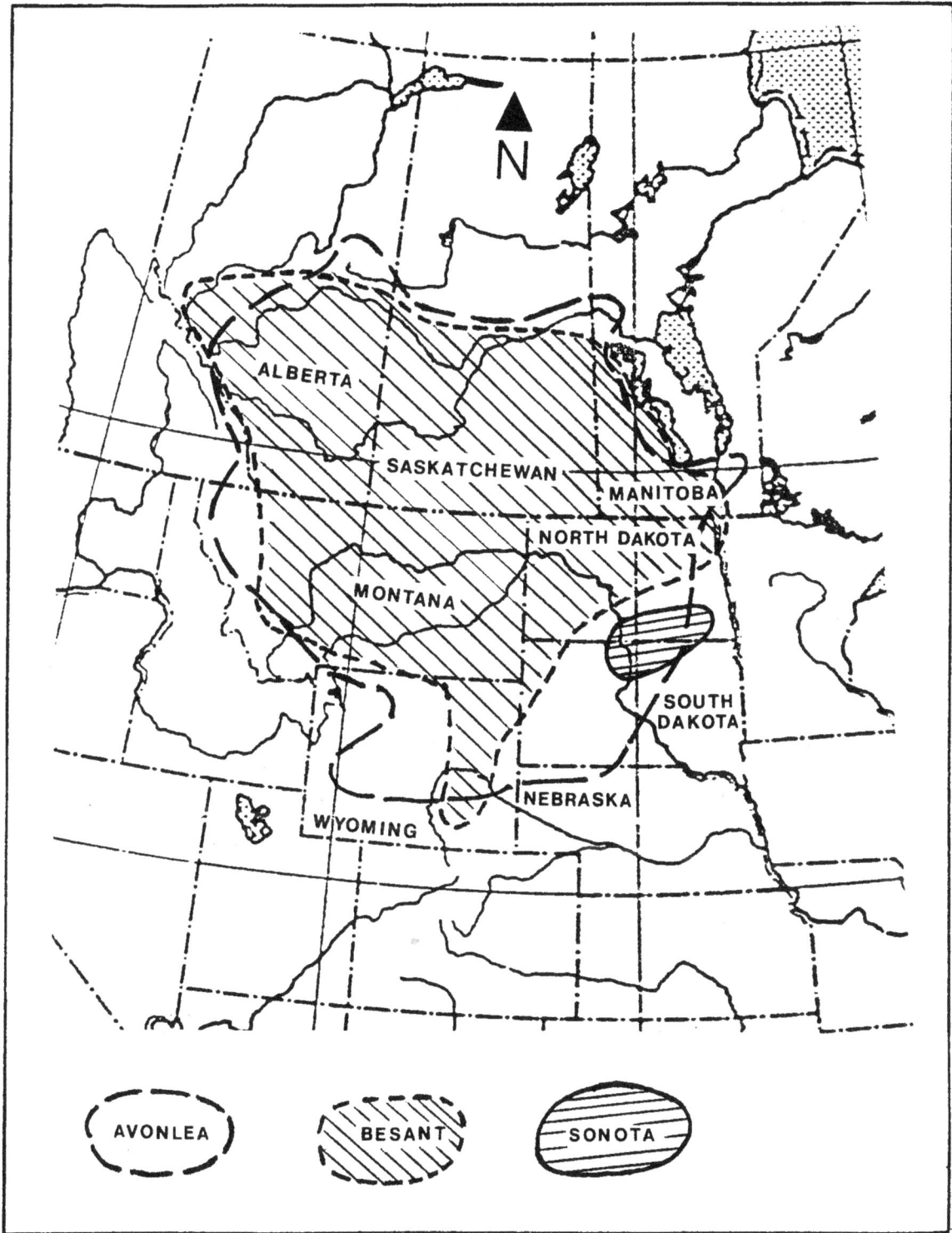

Figure 22. Map of the maximum territorial extents of Avonlea, Besant and Sonota archaeological remains.

1000. This whole *chrono-geographic* picture suggests the retreat of one ethno-linguistic group (the Besant Phase) to the west and then to the south in the face of expansion by another ethno-linguistic group, the Old Women's Phase. I suggest the equation of the Besant Phase with the Apacheans, and the Old Women's Phase with the ancestors of the Blackfoot.

The Avonlea Phase, which co-existed for so long with the Besant Phase, on the basis of Morlan's data seems to co-exist with the Old Women's Phase for a period of about 150 to 200 years, but then also disappears from the territories claimed by the Old Women's Phase. The Avonlea Phase's latest survival is west of the Rocky Mountains in the Kootenai Basin (Morlan 1988:295), where Reeves (1983:20) interprets it as being ancestral to the Kutenai ethno-linguistic group that occupied the area historically.

The above scenario flies in the face of *in situ* development theories for the origin of the Old Women's Phase that have long dominated archaeological thinking in the northwestern Great Plains, and no doubt it will be bitterly criticized in some quarters. Certainly, the geographic replacement scenario needs to be filled out in detail and those details critically examined before it can be accepted as more than a promising new interpretation.

The scenario of a Besant/Apachean retreat southward into Montana ca. A.D. 800 suggests that the break-off of linguistic contact between the Apacheans and their Athapaskan cousins in the western Boreal Forest should date to that time. Hoijer's (1956:231) glottochronological study of the Athapaskan languages suggests a divergence between the Apachean group and the Boreal Forest Athapaskan languages between 1000 and 700 years ago, or between A.D. 900 and 1200. Dates of acquisition for the linguistic materials used by Hoijer range between ca. A.D. 1870 and 1930, giving A.D. 1900 as the approximate modern date from which to count backwards.

However, Hymes (1957:293), as a result of his critique of Hoijer's calculations, uses the same data base to produce glottochronological divergences between the two groups of 1300 to 1000 years ago, or between ca. A.D. 600 and 900. Clearly, Hymes' dating range for the break-off of the Apachean languages fits quite well with the suggested Besant withdrawal to the south.

The last radiocarbon-dated Besant Phase remains are found within the Missouri drainage basin in Montana (Morlan 1988:295). About A.D. 1000 the Besant Phase disappears as an archaeological entity, that is the diagnostic projectile point types are no longer manufactured. Subsequent projectile points are small, side-notched arrow points. To the north, in Alberta, Saskatchewan and northern Montana, such points are named Prairie Side-notched and associated with the Old Women's Phase, i.e., the Blackfoot ancestors. South of the Missouri River in Montana and northern Wyoming there is no clearly defined phase or complex to which such

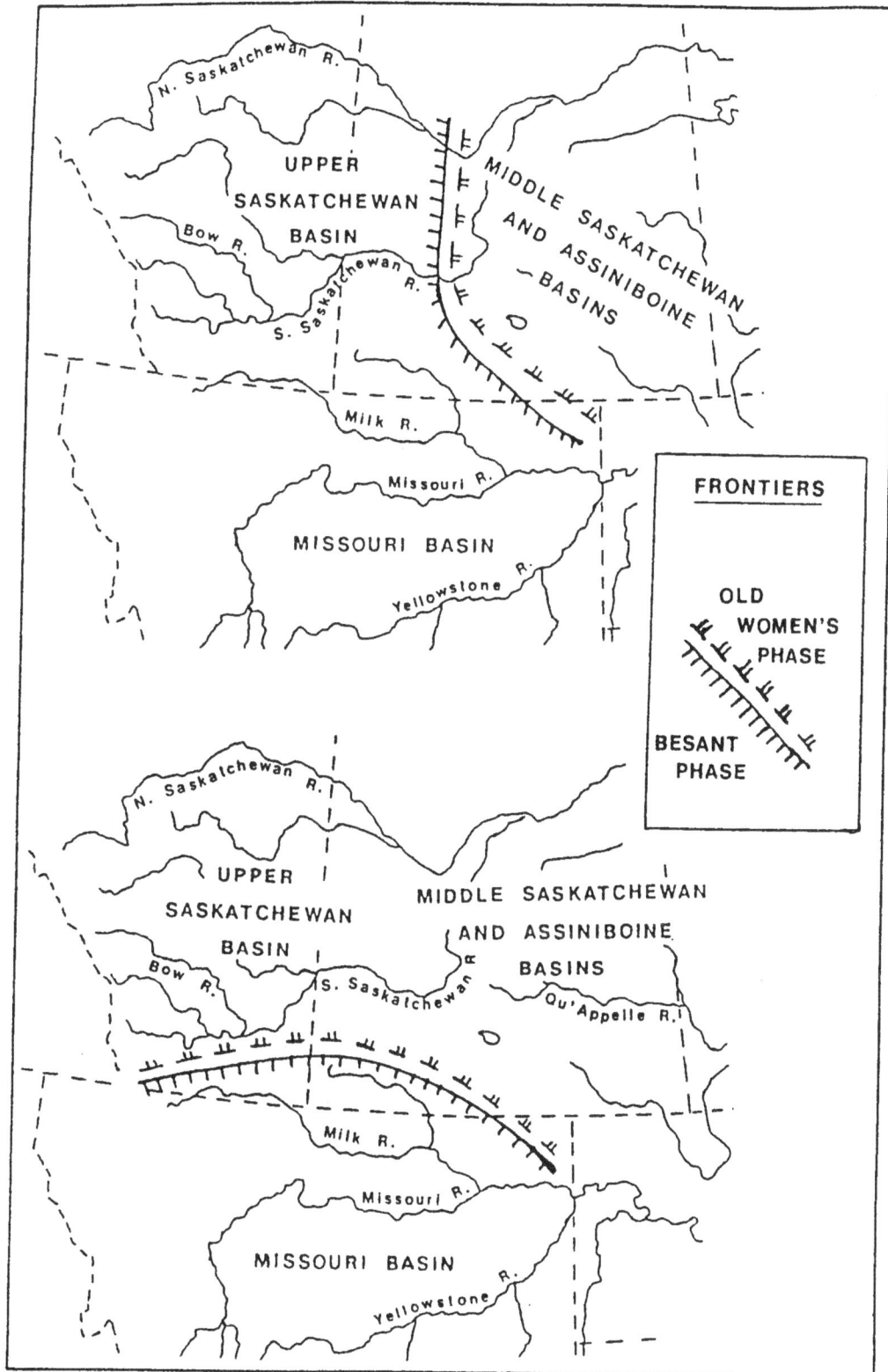

Figure 23. Maps of the frontiers between the Besant Phase and the Old Women's Phase, around
A.D. 700 (top) and around A.D. 800 (bottom).

47

points can be assigned at present. The general summaries available to me tend to pass very quickly and with minimal comment over the period of time between A.D. 800 and 1500. In archaeological writing this is a typical symptom of a limited data base and a lack of data synthesis, as is explicitly acknowledged by Greiser (1994:46).

I suggest that the Apacheans, who I postulate as living in the central-southern Montana/northern Wyoming area ca. A.D. 800-1200, gradually abandoned the production of Besant Phase diagnostic projectile points between A.D. 800 and 1000 in favor of the newer side-notched style used by their northern neighbors.

THE SHELL RIVER HOMELAND

Farrer (1991:196) notes a Mescalero Apache tradition that they used to live far to the north at a place they called the Shell River, which is identified with the Yellowstone River of southern Montana by Farrer. The reference to "shell" in the name is probably to freshwater mussels that are present in Missouri basin rivers, such as the present-day Mussellshell River of central Montana. I submit that it is no mere coincidence that the Yellowstone River's drainage basin contains many of the rock art sites showing the four-pointed star and heartline motifs.

Keyser (1975) has attributed all shield-bearing warrior rock art motifs on the northern Great Plains to Shoshonean-speakers, supposed to have borrowed the motif from the Fremont Culture of Utah. As Loendorf (1990:51-52) points out, Keyser's arrival time in Montana for the Shoshoneans of ca. A.D. 1300-1400 is too late to account for Loendorf's dated shield-bearers in southern Montana (ca. A.D. 1100). Loendorf offers the alternative suggestion that these earlier shield-bearers were painted by Athapaskans. In turn, Magne and Klassen (1991:415) have questioned Loendorf's Athapaskan interpretation on the basis that "Northern Athapaskan culture areas have very little in the way of a rock art tradition and certainly no shield-bearing warrior antecedents."

The Magne-Klassen position is rather weak in that it seems to assume that ethnic groups do not learn from one another, an assumption well known to be completely untenable. I suggest that Keyser's ultimate attribution of the shield-bearing warrior motif to the Fremont Culture is correct, but that it was the Athapaskan-speaking Apacheans rather than Shoshoneans who brought the motif onto the northern Great Plains.

My reasoning is this: a population withdrawal of Besant/Apacheans from their northern territories in Alberta and Saskatchewan would likely eventually result in an expansion elsewhere. One direction of expansion of hunting territories might be into southwestern Wyoming and beyond into the eastern Great Basin. A movement in this direction between A.D. 800 and 1000

48

would result in an encounter with the contemporaneous Fremont Culture (Figure 24). Shield depictions and shield-warriors are already present in the Classic Vernal Style of Fremont rock art in northeastern Utah at that time (Schaafsma 1980:168-175). These well-developed shield and shield-warrior motifs suggest a possible aggressive character to the Fremont Culture, perhaps extending to internecine warfare among the Fremont themselves. Under such social conditions, an intruding ethnic group might find their hunting parties coming under attack. I visualize some such interaction occurring between the Apacheans and the Uinta Fremont (the local variant located in northeastern Utah). This could easily have resulted in the transfer of warfare-related items such as shield-making and rock art to the Apacheans. This same hostile interaction may have stimulated technological innovations, such as the use of bison-hide for shields and the improvement of the bow through the addition of sinew-backing.

Schaafsma (1980:175) also notes the presence of the "weeping eye" motif in the Classic Vernal Style, a motif also seen in the rock art of Montana and Wyoming (see Figure 9) and which probably represents face-paint worn by warriors and/or ceremonialists.

I have already suggested changes in Apachean culture such as the adoption of a side-notched projectile point style and the heartline motif from the Old Women's Phase to the north. The acceptance of shields and shield-warrior rock art from the Fremont would be congruent with this, in that it would suggest an open-minded world view. Later cultural borrowing, after the arrival of the Apacheans in the Southwest, is well-known although "the basic ideas and the content were reworked to harmonize with Apachean conceptions and purposes" (Opler 1983:380). In keeping with this, the four-pointed star motif was either developed at this time by the Apacheans themselves, or possibly borrowed from some other group with whom they were in contact: perhaps with possible Pawnee-ancestors to the southeast in the central Great Plains.

THE SECOND MOVE SOUTH

If the Apacheans appear in southeastern Colorado, on the doorstep to the Southwest culture area, at about A.D. 1350 - as suggested at the beginning of this study - then they probably began moving south from central Wyoming around A.D. 1200 or 1250. And I visualize them as moving south through eastern Colorado. The main reason for favoring this route, rather than one west of the Rocky Mountains, is that the earliest historically known Apacheans are plains-adapted peoples, with a subsistence base focused on bison-hunting. If my speculations above are correct, this subsistence base was a traditional one for them - going back to ca. 100 B.C., at least.

A number of questions can be posed at this point: why would the Apacheans leave the Shell River homeland?, how were they able to occupy a new territory to the south that presumably already had a human population?, and what impact did they have on these local human populations?

Farrer (1991:196) reports the tradition among the Mescalero Apache of what is called the Shell River Prophecy, that was given to them on the Shell River (the Yellowstone River):

> The event occurred during the time the people who became known as the Mescalero Apache were migrating into the Southwest. The holy man appeared to be dead, only to manifest life again on the fourth day. It developed that he had been on a spirit journey to The Real World where he learned, and shared much that was of importance to the Apache people at that time; he also delivered a prophecy that provided information about what was to occur in the future and that assisted the Mescalero in finding and recognizing their new homelands as they were traveling south...

Farrer gives no details, but a prophecy of this sort could very well become self-fulfilling, in that it could start or predispose a nomadic people to move in a certain direction, i.e., to the south. Unfortunately, there is no way of proving that such a prophecy *was* a root cause of the second stage of the Apachean migration.

Did some other ethnic group, or groups, push them south? It seems possible that after the first retreat south, the Apacheans may have still been under pressure from the north from the Old Women's Phase people. However, there is no developed data base relating to this possibility at present. And if the Apacheans were being intruded upon, it was probably *not* by the Siouan-speaking Crows, as the Crows do not seem to appear in the Montana/Wyoming area until about A.D. 1400-1500 (Frison 1979).

A more likely candidate is the Fremont Culture, which disappears from Utah about A.D. 1200-1300. The various models advanced to describe Fremont prehistory have been summarized by Anderson (1983). It seems generally agreed now that earlier models asserting an *in situ* development from the Fremont Culture into the historically-known Shoshoneans of the Great Basin are no longer tenable due to a lack of continuity in material culture, backed up by linguistic evidence internal to the Shoshonean languages.

Aikens' conception that the Fremont peoples were Athapaskan-speakers, while not generally popular, has been reasserted by Aikens and Witherspoon (1986:14). I do not find it convincing, especially since there is newly developed DNA evidence based upon 47 human burials which "effectively precludes Athapaskan ancestry" for the population of the Great Salt Lake variant of the Fremont Culture (Parr *et al.* 1996:514).

Anderson (1983:23-26) presents what he calls a "composite model" of Fremont cultural history that visualizes a termination of the Fremont Culture through at least partial assimilation by the eastward-advancing Shoshoneans. Could, then, some sort of Shoshonean-Fremont composite have advanced upon the Apacheans from the eastern Great Basin?

The nature and distribution of archaeological remains in Wyoming that are identified as Shoshonean are discussed by Frison (1971:280-281) and Hoefer *et al.* (1992:64-66). While there is one radiocarbon date as early as A.D. 1260, most early dates for Shoshonean remains in western Wyoming are between A.D. 1350 and 1400. This seems too late to qualify Shoshoneans as an "initial cause" for Apachean withdrawal.

However, this does not completely dispose of the Fremont Culture. It is by no means certain that all Fremont peoples were assimilated by the in-coming Shoshoneans. Indeed, Butler (1983) has summarized data indicating an "attenuated" Fremont presence along the Snake River in southern Idaho to perhaps as late as A.D. 1600. Ultimately, however, the ethno-linguistic identity of the peoples of the Fremont Culture is still open to debate.

I suggest here that the Kiowas are a possible candidate for identification with at least some northern populations of the Fremont Culture. This is based in part upon the Kiowa tradition of their earliest homeland (Mooney 1898:153):

> The earliest historic tradition of the Kiowa locates them in or beyond the mountains at the extreme sources of the Yellowstone and the Missouri, in what is now western Montana. They describe it as a region of great cold and deep snows, and say that they had the Flatheads...near them, and that on the other side of the mountains was a large stream flowing westward, evidently an upper branch of the Columbia [or, perhaps, the Snake River?]. These mountains they still call *Gai K'op*, "Kiowa Mountains".

Harrington (1939) has further discussed these Kiowa traditions, and the historical documentation of the Kiowas' eventual migration south from the Montana/Wyoming area in the early A.D. 1800s is discussed by John (1985). Some archaeologists have incorrectly attempted to link the Kiowa to prehistoric archaeological remains in the Southwest culture area (e.g., Jelinek 1967:162-163).

Note that the oldest traditional homeland for the Kiowas, the Missouri headwaters area of southwestern Montana, is readily entered from the south - following the same route as Interstate Highway 15 - through Monida Pass from the eastern Snake River basin of Idaho. This pass is a very easy crossing of the Rocky Mountains. I therefore suggest a possible northern movement from eastern Idaho of a portion of the Fremont population, to become the ancestors of the Kiowas. Once established among the Missouri headwaters, they might have exerted some pressure on the Apacheans to the east. However, this all remains highly speculative until such time as sufficient evidence can be assembled to test these ideas. Note, however, that contacts between the Apacheans and the Kiowas on the northern Great Plains are demonstrated through the close historic association of the Kiowa and Kiowa Apaches.

So far, convincing evidence for a "push" from another ethnic group to start a second southward retreat by the Apacheans cannot be brought forward. Perhaps, then, there was some factor that drew their camps ever farther south, such as better hunting conditions or an abandonment of eastern Colorado by its previous inhabitants?

Between about A.D. 1000 and 1300 an archaeological complex known as the Upper Republican Culture occupied hamlets in stream valleys of southwestern Nebraska and northwestern Kansas (Figure 24). These people are thought to be ancestral, at least in part, to the historic Pawnee and Arikara (Ubelaker and Jantz 1979). They had a mixed economy of agriculture, gathering and hunting (Wedel 1986). At this same time northeastern Colorado as far west as the Rocky Mountain foothills was utilized by people using Upper Republican pottery and projectile points, probably during bison hunting expeditions from the hamlets farther east, in a subsistence pattern similar to that known for the historic Pawnee (Cassells 1983:170-173; Wedel 1936:57-62; Eighmy 1994:233-237).

The above scenario has been disputed recently, some authors suggesting that the western campsites belong to a local population, rather than being a peripheral Upper Republican phenomenon (see discussion in Bozell 1995:155-156).

However this may be, about A.D. 1250-1275 the Upper Republican hamlets were abandoned and, simultaneously, Upper Republican remains cease to appear in Colorado. This is interpreted as a withdrawal eastwards by these peoples. A suggested cause of the abandonment has been climatic change resulting in lowered temperatures and decreased rainfall unfavorable to maize agriculture (Wedel 1986:132-133). This interpretation has been challenged by Blakeslee (1993), who presents evidence favoring swidden-agriculture exhaustion of soil fertility as the cause. However it was caused, such a withdrawal of Upper Republican hunters from northeastern Colorado would have created an opportunity for southern expansion by the Apacheans.

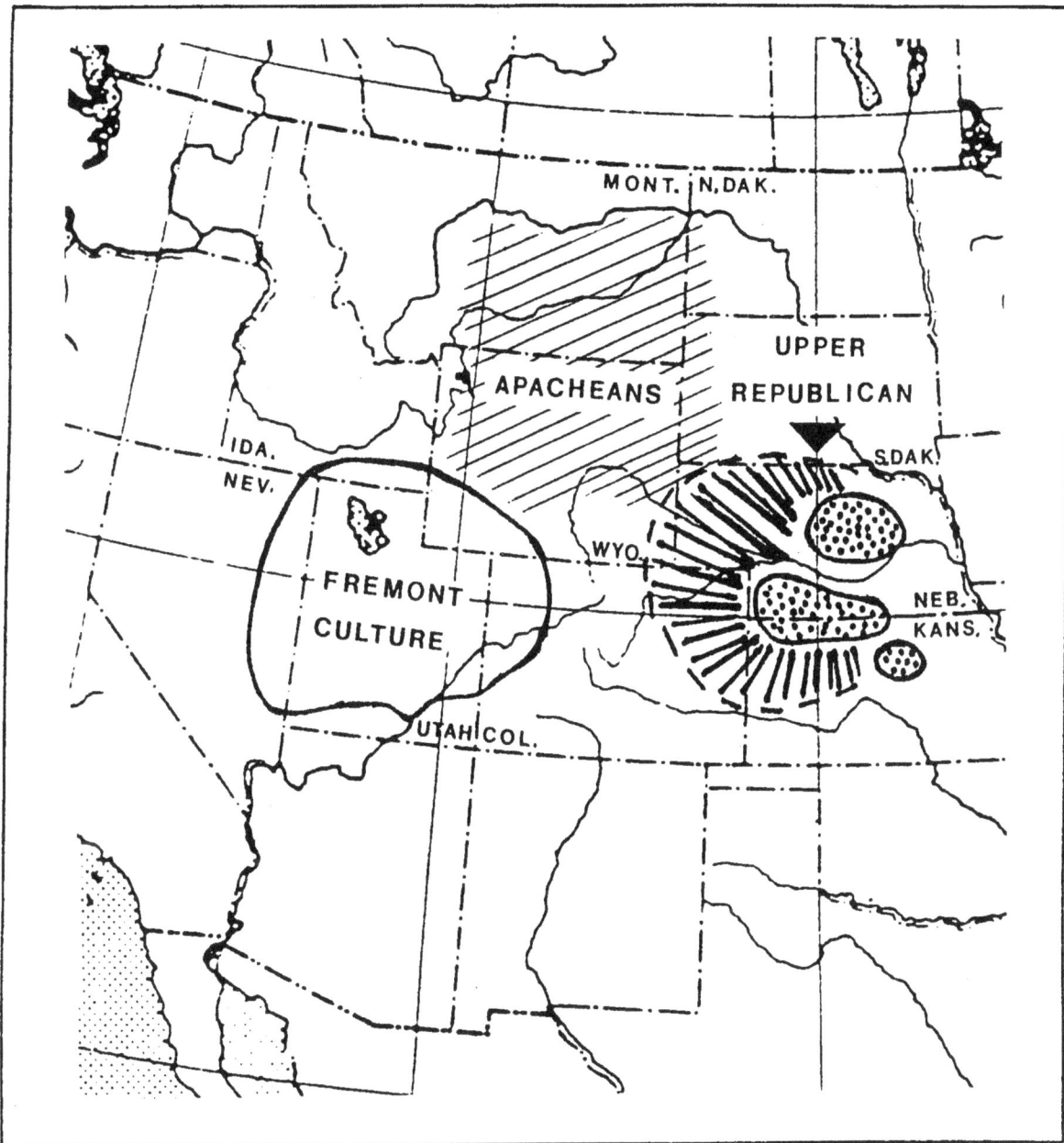

Figure 24. Map showing the approximate locations of the Fremont culture, the Apacheans, and the Upper Republican variants, around A.D. 900 to 1300. Stippled ovals in the Upper Republican area are areas of hamlet settlement, around which radiating lines indicate the inferred extent of bison-hunting zones for those hamlets.

Was there any change in bison populations in eastern Colorado that could have attracted the Apacheans? This question is posed because, for the Southern Plains (parts of Texas, Oklahoma, and New Mexico), Dillehay (1974:183-185) proposes that there was a period of bison absence (A.D. 500 to 1200/1300), followed by a period of bison presence (A.D. 1200/1300 to 1550). Dillehay interprets these periods as meaning there was a climatic shift about A.D. 1200/1300 that favored an increase in bison populations on the Southern Plains, while at the same time discouraging agriculture in the drier western portions. If the same pattern is present for eastern Colorado, it might explain an Apachean southward movement.

Various problems exist with Dillehay's model of bison presence/absence, beginning with his having overlooked then-published data relevant to the problem, the existence of contradictory new data, and the problem that his terms "presence" and "absence" are over-generalizations that would have better been replaced by terms such as "relatively high abundance" and "relatively low abundance". Those critiques aside, however, the question here is whether these periods also apply to eastern Colorado? Butler has studied the matter, and concludes that *bison are present during both periods* in eastern Colorado and there is no discernable change in this presence at A.D. 1200/1300 (1992:8-11). Thus, present data do not support climatic or animal population changes as causative factors in starting an Apachean movement south.

So far in the discussion, the only promising causal factor for a southward movement ca. A.D. 1200/1250 by the Apacheans seems to be the circumstantial withdrawal of Central Plains Tradition hunters from northeastern Colorado. Occupation of that area by Apacheans might have placed them within easy raiding distance of the Central Plains hamlets, thus hastening the withdrawal of the Central Plains population.

Such a southern advance would also bring the Apacheans into direct contact with the semi-agricultural population of southeastern Colorado, the Apishapa Phase of possible Caddoan affiliation that ends ca. A.D. 1350/1400 (Cassells 1983:173-177; Baugh 1994:277-279). While the exact nature of Apachean impact is unclear, the complete termination of the Apishapa cultural tradition in southeastern Colorado suggests either extinction, absorption, or expulsion. If we assume that the Apacheans were well-armed with superior weaponry - sinew-backed bows and bison-hide shields - and probably had a much larger population base, then the Apishapa Phase people could have been overwhelmed in a relatively short time.

54

8

FINAL SUMMATION

The above study argues that when the Athapaskan-speaking Apacheans arrived in the Southwestern culture area, ca. A.D. 1350-1400, they brought with them a hunting-warfare complex consisting of (1) the sinew-backed bow, (2) the mountain lion-skin quiver, (3) the bison-hide shield, (4) the four-pointed star motif, and (5) the heartline motif.

The archaeological evidence cited herein suggests the widespread adoption of the first four elements of the complex by the Pueblo Indians between A.D. 1400 and 1500. The fifth element, the heartline motif, found lasting acceptance only among the Zunis, but during the A.D. 1800s experienced a second expansion among the Pueblo Indians due to Zuni influence.

Finally, the study briefly outlines a scenario for the southern migrations of Apacheans from the northwestern Great Plains to the Southwest. Many details of this scenario remain to be worked out and tested, and no doubt many corrections made. I look forward to seeing these emerge in the years to come.

APPENDIX A

A list of pre-A.D. 1330 evidences for archaeological bows and illustrations of bows in the Southwest, as shown in Figure 4.

ARCHAEOLOGICAL BOW REMAINS

SOUTHERN NEVADA/NORTHWESTERN ARIZONA:

Gypsum Cave, Nevada: one fragment (Harrington 1933:127-128).
Heaton Cave, Arizona: Pueblo II-Pueblo III, a whole bow (Judd 1926:148, Plate 53a).

WESTERN ANASAZI (NORTHEASTERN ARIZONA/SOUTHEASTERN UTAH):

Poncho House, Utah: Pueblo III, one bow (Guernsey 1931:99, 107).
Cave 1, Tsegi Canyon: Pueblo I, one bow (Guernsey 1931:99).
Antelope House, Canyon de Chelly: Pueblo III, fragments of 14 bows, one fragmentary "ceremonial bow" (Magers 1986:285-287).
Prayer Rock Caves, Chuska Mountains: Basketmaker III, one whole, six fragmentary bows (Morris 1980:124-125).

CENTRAL ANASAZI (MESA VERDE, SAN JUAN, CHACO CANYON):

Unidentified Cliff Dwelling, Mesa Verde: Pueblo III, two whole bows (Nordenskiöld 1893:101).
Painted Kiva House, Mesa Verde: Pueblo III, two fragments of bows (Nordenskiöld 1893:101, Plate 43).
Aztec Ruin, New Mexico: Pueblo II-Pueblo III, one bow fragment (Morris 1919:60).
Pueblo Bonito, Chaco Canyon: Pueblo II, two bows (Judd 1954:248-249).
Pueblo del Arroyo, Chaco Canyon: Pueblo II, one bow fragment (Judd 1959:130).

UPPER GILA/MIMBRES AREA:

Tularosa Phase Cliff Dwelling, Mogollon Mountains: 94 (+?) bows (Hibben 1938).
Bat Cave: pre-A.D. 1100, one bow fragment (Dick 1965:83).
Tularosa/Cordova Caves: Reserve-Tularosa Phases, two bows (Martin *et al.* 1952:339-340, 382, 384, 386).
Various Upper Gila Caves: many bow remains (Cosgrove 1947:61-62).
Other Upper Gila Caves: Pinelawn through Tularosa Phases, fragments of seven bows (Martin, Rinaldo, and Bluhm 1954:183, 185, 187-189).

PRE-A.D. 1300 ILLUSTRATIONS OF BOWS (ROCK ART, MURALS, CERAMICS)

SOUTHWESTERN UTAH (ANASAZI):

Clark Canyon Site: rock art, D-shaped bow with arrow (Steward 1941:326).
Site 130, Oak Canyon: rock art, three archers with D-shaped bows, two isolated D-shaped bows (Steward 1941:Plate 48).

FREMONT CULTURE SITES (EASTERN UTAH/WESTERN COLORADO):

Sieber Canyon, Colorado: petroglyph archer with D-shaped bow (Wormington and Lister 1956:123).
Various sites in Nine Mile Canyon, Utah: petroglyphs, five archers with D-shaped bows, three archers with oval bows (Schaafsma 1971:30-35, Figure 33, Plate 16; Schaafsma 1980:177).
Poison Springs Canyon, Utah: petroglyphs, one archer with D-shaped bow and arrow, one archer with arc-shaped bow and arrow (Castleton 1978:137-138).
Fremont River, Utah: petroglyphs, two archers with D-shaped bows, one archer with arc-shaped bow (Castleton 1978:153, 156, 158).
Moab Area, Utah: petroglyphs, four archers with D-shaped bows (Castleton 1978:189-190).

GLEN CANYON AREA, SOUTHERN UTAH (ANASAZI): the examples listed immediately below are petroglyphs of Turner's Style 4 (Pueblo II-III) for the Glen Canyon Area.

NA 7179, Lower Cha Canyon: two archers with D-shaped bows (Turner 1963:Figure 13).
NA 6423, West Creek Canyon: an archer with bow and arrow (Turner 1963:Figure 34).
NA 7147, Paiute Creek: archer with D-shaped bow (Turner 1963:Figure 39).
NA 6281, North Side of San Juan River: one archer with D-shaped bow, arrow and quiver, second archer with D-shaped bow (Turner 1963:Figure 85).

NA 7421, mouth of Desha Canyon: isolated D-shaped bow and arrow (Turner 1963:Figure 68).

MARSH PASS, NORTHEASTERN ARIZONA (ANASAZI):

Kinboko Canyon: petroglyph of hump-backed archer shooting D-shaped bow and arrow (Kidder and Guernsey 1919:195, Plate 94c).

SOUTHEASTERN UTAH:

Mouth of Butler Wash: archer with D-shaped bow and arrow (Castleton 1979:223).
Site # 4, Horse Canyon, Canyonlands National Park: Fremont (?) white pictograph of shield-bearer with D-shaped bow and arrow (Castleton 1979:281).

MESA VERDE, SOUTHWESTERN COLORADO (ANASAZI):

Fire Temple, Chapin Mesa: two red-on-white pictographs of archers with D-shaped bows, Pueblo III (Schaafsma 1980:142).
New Fire House, Chapin Mesa: two red-on-white pictographs of archers with arc-shaped bows, Pueblo III (Smith 1952:60).
M.V. 687, Chapin Mesa: petroglyph archer holding a D-shaped bow (Rohn 1977:123).
Unidentified Cliff Dwelling: Pueblo III Black-on-white bowl sherd with design of hump-backed archer shooting a D-shaped bow and arrow at an animal (Nordenskiöld 1893:108).
Unidentified provenience: Chapin Black-on-white bowl with archer shooting a D-shaped bow and arrow at a mother bear and cub, Basketmaker III (Brody 1991:Figure 17).
Unidentified site: Piedra Black-on-white bowl with hump-backed archer hunting ducks with D-shaped bow and arrow, Pueblo I (Brody 1991:Figure 19).

PIEDRA DISTRICT, SOUTHWESTERN COLORADO (ANASAZI):

Site 5AA91: Rosa Black-on-white potsherd with arms of an archer holding a D-shaped bow and arrow, Pueblo I (Adams and Adams 1979:25, 30).

NAVAJO RESERVOIR DISTRICT, NORTHWESTERN NEW MEXICO (ANASAZI):

LA 3015: petroglyph archer with D-shaped bow and arrow, and isolated D-shaped bow and arrow (Schaafsma 1963:10, 13).
LA 3042: petroglyph archer with D-shaped bow (Schaafsma 1963:15).

LA 4072: two petroglyph archers with oval-shaped bows (Schaafsma 1963:20).
LA 4398: petroglyph archer with D-shaped bow and arrow (Schaafsma 1963:23).
RA-6, Largo Canyon: petroglyph archer with oval-shaped bow (Schaafsma 1975:10).

CHACO CANYON, NEW MEXICO (ANASAZI):

Site 400: petroglyph archer with D-shaped bow and arrow, Pueblo II - Pueblo III (Steed 1980:50-51).
Bc-51: white pictographs on wall of Kiva 6 of three archers with D-shaped bows (Brody 1991:61).
Mockingbird Canyon: red pictograph of archer with D-shaped bow (Brody 1991:62).

HOHOKAM CULTURE, SOUTHERN ARIZONA:

Picture Rocks, Tucson Mountains: three petroglyph isolated D-shaped bows, Gila Petroglyph Style (Schaafsma 1980:88, 95).
South Mountains: petroglyph archer with D-shaped bow, Gila Petroglyph Style (Schaafsma 1980:93).
Snaketown Site: archer with D-shaped bow on Sacaton red-on-buff sherd, and archer with D-shaped bow on Gila Butte Red-on-buff sherd (Haury 1976:241).

MIMBRES CERAMICS, SOUTHWESTERN NEW MEXICO (MOGOLLON):

Galaz Ruin: 1) bowl showing centipede holding five D-shaped bows with right legs, five arrows with left legs; 2) bowl showing archer shooting bears with D-shaped bow (Anyon and Leblanc 1984:516, 547).
Mattocks Site: bowl showing D-shaped bow and two arrows (Brody et al. 1983:72).
Oldtown Ruin, Osborn Collection: 1) bowl showing three hunters each holding a D-shaped bow and arrow, 2) bowl showing two men with a D-shaped bow (Fewkes 1914:24, 27).
Unknown Provenience: 1) bowl showing an oval bow and two arrows, 2) bowl showing an archer holding a D-shaped bow and an arrow 3) bowl showing hunter wearing a deer's head and holding a D-shaped bow and arrow (Brody et al. 1983:94, 96, 98).
Unknown Provenience, Osborn Collection: bowl showing seated archer with D-shaped bowl and three arrows, plus other figures (Fewkes 1923:27).

NORTHERN CHIHUAHUA:

Candelaria Site: petroglyphs of five archers with D-shaped or oval-shaped bows (Davis 1980:50-51).

REFERENCES CITED

Adams, E. Charles, and Jenny L. Adams
1979   Ceramic Life Forms in the Lower Piedra District, Colorado, and Their Relationship to Life Forms in the Upper San Juan Region. *Southwestern Lore* 45(3):25-38.

Aikens, C. Melvin, and Younger T. Witherspoon
1986   Great Basin Numic Prehistory: Linguistics, Archeology, and Environment. In *Anthropology of the Desert West: Essays in Honor of Jesse D. Jennings*, edited by Carol J. Condie and Don D. Fowler, pp. 7-20. Anthropological Papers No. 110, University of Utah, Salt Lake City.

Anderson, Duane C.
1983   Models of Fremont Culture History: An Evaluation. In *Prairie Archaeology: Papers in Honor of David A. Baerreis*, edited by Guy E. Gibbon, pp. 15-28. Publications in Anthropology No. 3, University of Minnesota, Minneapolis.

Anonymous
1961   Regional Pictograph Styles. *Wyoming Archaeologist* 4(11):2-13.

Anyon, Roger, and Steven A. LeBlanc
1984   *The Galaz Ruin.* University of New Mexico Press, Albuquerque.

Badhorse, Beverly
1979   Petroglyphs - Possible Religious Significance of Some. *Wyoming Archaeologist* 22(3):18-30.

Baldwin, Stuart J.
1983   A Tentative Occupation Sequence for Abo Pass, Central New Mexico. *COAS* 1(2):12-28.

1986   The Mountain Lion in Tompiro Stone Art. In *By Hands Unknown: Papers on Rock Art and Archaeology in Honor of James G. Bain*, edited by Anne V. Poore, pp. 8-17. The Archaeological Society of New Mexico: 12.

1988a   Studies in Piro-Tompiro Ethnohistory and Western Tompiro Archaeology. Ms in possession of author.

1988b   Tompiro Culture, Subsistence and Trade. Ph.D Thesis, Department of Archaeology, University of Calgary, Calgary.

1992   Evidence for a Tompiro Morning Star Kachina. *The Artifact* 30(4):1-14.

Basso, Keith H. (editor)
1971   *Western Apache Raiding and Warfare.* University of Arizona Press, Tucson.

Baugh, Timothy G.
1994   Holocene Adaptations in the Southern High Plains. In *Plains Indians, A.D. 500-1500: The Archaeological Past of Historic Groups*, edited by Karl H. Schlesier, pp. 264-289. University of Oklahoma Press, Norman and London.

Berger, Rainer, and W.F. Libby
1968   UCLA Radiocarbon Dates VII. *Radiocarbon* 10(1):149-160.

Birdsall, W.R.
1891   The Cliff Dwellings of the Cañons of the Mesa Verde. *Bulletin of the American Geographical Society* 23(4):584-620.

Blakeslee, Donald J.
1993   Modelling the Abandonment of the Central Plains: Radiocarbon Dates and the Origin of the Initial Coalescent. *Plains Anthropologist* 38(145):199-214.

Bluhm, Elaine A., and Allen Liss
1961   The Anker Site. In *Chicago Area Archaeology*, edited by Elaine A. Bluhm, pp. 89-137. Bulletin 3, Illinois Archaeological Survey, Urbana.

Bourke, John Gregory
1884   *The Snake-Dance of the Moquis of Arizona.* Charles Scribner's Sons, New York.

Bozell, John R.
1995   Culture, Environment, and Bison Populations on the Late Prehistoric and Early Historic Central Plains. *Plains Anthropologist* 40(152):145-163.

Bradley, James H.
1923   Characteristics, Habits and Customs of the Blackfoot Indians. *Contributions to the Historical Society of Montana* 10:256-287.

Brasser, Ted J.
1978   Tipi Paintings, Blackfoot Style. In *Contextual Studies of Material Culture*, edited by David W. Zimmerly, pp. 7-18. Mercury Series Paper No. 43, Canadian Ethnology Service, National Museum of Man, Ottawa.

1979   The Pedigree of the Hugging Bear Tipi in the Blackfoot Camp. *American Indian Art Magazine* 5(1):32-39.

Bray, Robert T.
  1963   Southern Cult Motifs from the Utz Oneota Site, Saline County, Missouri. *The Missouri Archaeologist* 25:1-40.

Brody, J.J.
  1977   *Mimbres Painted Pottery*. School of American Research, Santa Fe and University of New Mexico Press, Albuquerque.

  1991   *Anasazi and Pueblo Painting*. University of New Mexico Press, Albuquerque.

Brody, J.J., Catherine J. Scott, Steven A. LeBlanc, and Tony Berlant
  1983   *Mimbres Pottery*. Hudson Hills Press, New York.

Brose, David S.
  1978   Late Prehistory of the Upper Great Lakes Area. In *Handbook of North American Indians, Volume 15: Northeast*, edited by Bruce G. Trigger and William C. Sturtevant, pp. 569-582. Smithsonian Institution, Washington, D.C.

Brugge, David M.
  1983   Apacheans in Plains Culture History. *Bulletin of the Oklahoma Anthropological Society* 32:107-114.

Bryan, Alan
  1967   The First People. In *Alberta: A Natural History*, edited by W.G. Hardy, pp. 277-293. M.G. Hurtig, Edmonton.

Bunzel, Ruth L.
  1929   *The Pueblo Potter*. Contributions to Anthropology 8, Columbia University, New York.

Butler, B. Robert
  1983   *The Quest for the Historic Fremont and A Guide to the Prehistoric Pottery of Southern Idaho*. Occasional Papers No. 33, Idaho Museum of Natural History, Pocatello.

Butler, William B.
  1992   Bison Presence and Absence in Colorado. *Southwestern Lore* 58(3):1-14.

Carbone, Gerald
  1972   An Amateur's General Surface Report of the Tongue River Drainage Area. *Wyoming Archaeologist* 15(4):6-46.

Carlson, Muriel
    1989   An Update on a Catlinite Pendant. *Saskatchewan Archaeological Society* 10(3):65-66.

Cassells, E. Steve
    1983   *The Archaeology of Colorado.* Johnson Books, Boulder.

Castleton, Kenneth B.
    1978   *Petroglyphs and Pictographs of Utah, Volume 1: The East and Northeast.* Utah Museum of Natural History, Salt Lake City.

    1979   *Petroglyphs and Pictographs of Utah, Volume 2: The South, Central, West and Northwest.* Utah Museum of Natural History, Salt Lake City.

Chamberlain, Von Del
    1982   *When Stars Came Down to Earth: Cosmology of the Skidi Pawnee Indians of North America.* Ballena Press, Los Altos, and Center for Archaeoastronomy, College Park.

Chapman, Kenneth M.
    1936   *The Pottery of Santo Domingo Pueblo.* Memoirs of the Laboratory of Anthropology, Volume 1. Santa Fe.

    1938   The Cave Pictographs of the Rito de los Frijoles. In *Pajarito Plateau and Its Ancient People*, by Edgar L. Hewett, pp. 138-148. University of New Mexico and School of American Research, Albuquerque.

    1970   *The Pottery of San Ildefonso Pueblo.* Monograph No. 28, School of American Research, Santa Fe.

Cosgrove, C.B.
    1947   *Caves of the Upper Gila and Hueco Areas in New Mexico and Texas.* Papers of the Peabody Museum of American Archaeology and Ethnology, Harvard University, 24(2). Cambridge.

Coues, Elliott (editor)
    1987   *The Expedition of Zebulon Montgomery Pike.* Two volumes. Dover Publications, Inc., New York.

Cushing, Frank Hamilton
    1883   Zuni Fetiches. In *Second Annual Report of the Bureau of Ethnology to the Secretary of the Smithsonian Institution, 1880-'81*, pp. 3-45. Washington, D.C.

1886 A Study of Pueblo Pottery as Illustrative of Zuni Culture Growth. *Fourth Annual Report of the Bureau of Ethnology to the Secretary of the Smithsonian Institution, 1882-'83*, pp. 467-521. Washington, D.C.

Davis, John V.
1980 The Candelaria Style: An Identifiable Rock Art Tradition of Northern Chihuahua. *The Artifact* 18(2):43-55.

Davis, John V., and Kay S. Toness
1974 *A Rock Art Inventory at Hueco Tanks State Park, Texas.* Special Report No. 12, El Paso Archaeological Society, El Paso.

Davis, Leslie B.
1982 Montana Archaeology and Radiocarbon Chronology: 1962-1981. *Archaeology in Montana* Special Issue No.3, Bozeman. Pp. 1-30.

Dewdney, Selwyn
1975 *The Sacred Scrolls of the Southern Ojibway.* University of Toronto Press, Toronto.

Dick, Herbert W.
1965 *Bat Cave.* Monograph No. 27, School of American Research, Santa Fe.

Dillehay, Tom D.
1974 Late Quaternary Bison Population Changes on the Southern Plains. *Plains Anthropologist* 19(65):180-196.

Driver, Harold E., and William C. Massey
1957 *Comparative Studies of North American Indians.* Transactions (new series) 47(2), American Philosophical Society, Philadelphia.

Drucker, Philip
1941 *Culture Element Distributions: XVII, Yuman-Piman.* University of California Anthropological Records 4(1). Berkeley.

Dutton, Bertha P.
1963 *Sun Father's Way: The Kiva Murals of Kuaua.* University of New Mexico Press, Albuquerque.

Eighmy, Jeffrey L.
1994 The Central High Plains: A Cultural Historical Summary. In *Plains Indians, A.D. 500-1500: The Archaeological Past of Historic Groups*, edited by Karl H. Schlesier, pp. 224-238. University of Oklahoma Press, Norman and London.

Ellis, Florence Hawley
    1959   Laguna Bows and Arrows. *El Palacio* 66(3):91.

Epp, Henry T., and Ian Dycke (editors)
    1983   *Tracking Ancient Hunters: Prehistoric Archaeology in Saskatchewan.* Saskatchewan Archaeological Society, Regina.

Ewers, John C.
    1982   The Awesome Bear in Plains Indian Art. *American Indian Art Magazine* 7(3):36-45.

Farrer, Claire R.
    1991   *Living Life's Circle: Mescalero Apache Cosmovision.* University of New Mexico Press, Albuquerque.

Farrer, Claire R., and Bernard Second
    1981   Living the Sky: Aspects of Mescalero Apache Ethnoastronomy. In *Archaeoastronomy in the Americas*, edited by Ray A. Williams, pp. 137-150. Anthropological Paper No. 22, Ballena Press, Los Altos.

Fewkes, Jesse Walter
    1914   *Archeology of the Lower Mimbres Valley, New Mexico.* Smithsonian Miscellaneous Collections, 63(10). Washington, D.C.

    1923   *Designs on Prehistoric Pottery from the Mimbres Valley, New Mexico.* Smithsonian Miscellaneous Collections, 74(6). Washington, D.C.

Fletcher, Alice C., and Francis La Flesche
    1911   The Omaha Tribe. In *Twenty-Seventh Annual Report of the Bureau of American Ethnology to the Secretary of the Smithsonian Institution, 1905-1906*, pp. 17-642. Washington, D.C.

Forbes, Jack D.
    1959   Unknown Athapaskans: The Identification of the Jano, Jocome, Jumano, Manso, Suma, and Other Indian Tribes of the Southwest. *Ethnohistory* 6(2):97-159.

Fowler, Melvin L., and Robert L. Hall
    1978   Late Prehistory of the Illinois Area. In *Handbook of North American Indians, Volume 15: Northeast*, edited by Bruce G. Trigger and William C. Sturtevant, pp. 560-568. Smithsonian Institution, Washington, D.C.

Frison, George
    1970   The Kobold Site, 24BH406: A Post-Altithermal Record of Buffalo-Jumping for the Northwestern Plains. *Plains Anthropologist* 15(47):1-35.

1971   Shoshonean Antelope Procurement in the Upper Green River Basin, Wyoming. *Plains Anthropologist* 16(54):258-284.

1978   *Prehistoric Hunters of the High Plains*. Academic Press, New York.

1979   The Crow Indian Occupation of the High Plains: The Archaeological Evidence. *Archaeology in Montana* 20(3):3-16.

Gebhard, David
1966   The Shield Motif in Plains Rock Art. *American Antiquity* 31(5):721-732.

Gifford, E.W.
1933   *The Cocopa*. University of California Publications in American Archaeology and Ethnology 31(5). Berkeley.

1940   *Culture Element Distributions: XII Apache-Pueblo*. University of California Anthropological Records 4(1). Berkeley.

Gifford, James C.
1980   *Archaeological Explorations in Caves of the Point of Pines Region, Arizona*. Anthropological Papers of the University of Arizona No. 36. Tucson.

Greiser, Sally T.
1994   Late Prehistoric Cultures on the Montana Plains. In *Plains Indians, A.D. 500-1500: The Archaeological Past of Historic Groups*, edited by Karl H. Schlesier, pp. 34-55. University of Oklahoma Press, Norman and London.

Griffin, James B.
1978   Late Prehistory of the Ohio Valley. In *Handbook of North American Indians, Volume 15: Northeast*, edited by Bruce G. Trigger and William C. Sturtevant, pp. 547-559. Smithsonian Institution, Washington, D.C.

Grinnell, George Bird
1901   The Lodges of the Blackfeet. *American Anthropologist* 3(4):650-668.

1972   *The Cheyenne Indians*. University of Nebraska Press, Lincoln.

Griswold, Gillett
1970   Aboriginal Patterns of Trade Between the Columbia Basin and the Northern Plains. *Archaeology in Montana* 11(2-3):1-96.

Guernsey, Samuel J.
1931   *Explorations in Northeastern Arizona*. Papers of the Peabody Museum of American Archaeology and Ethnology, Harvard University, 12(1). Cambridge.

Habgood, Thelma
    1967   Petroglyphs and Pictographs in Alberta. *Archaeological Society of Alberta Newsletter* 13-14:1-40.

Habicht-Mauche, Judith A.
    1992   Coronado's Querechos and Teyas in the Archaeological Record of the Texas Panhandle. *Plains Anthropologist* 37(140):247-259.

Haile, Berard
    1947   *Starlore Among the Navaho.* Museum of Navajo Ceremonial Art, Santa Fe.

Hall, H.U.
    1926   Some Shields of the Plains and Southwest. *The Museum Journal* 17:36-61.

Hamilton, T.M.
    1982   *Native American Bows.* 2nd edition. Special Publications No. 5, Missouri Archaeological Society, Columbia.

Hammond, George P., and Agapito Rey
    1953   *Don Juan de Oñate, Colonizer of New Mexico, 1595-1628.* Coronado Cuarto Centennial Publications Vols. 5 and 6, University of New Mexico, Albuquerque.

Harrington, John P.
    1939   Kiowa Memories of the Northland. In *So Live the Works of Men*, edited by Donald D. Brand and Fred E. Harvey, pp. 162-176. University of New Mexico Press, Albuquerque.

Harrington, Mark Raymond
    1933   *Gypsum Cave, Nevada.* Southwest Museum Papers No. 8. Highland Park, Los Angeles, California.

Haskell, J. Loring
    1987   *Southern Athapaskan Migration, A.D. 200-1750.* Navajo Community College Press, Tsaile.

Haury, Emil W.
    1950   *The Stratigraphy and Archaeology of Ventana Cave.* University of Arizona Press, Tucson, and University of New Mexico Press, Albuquerque.

    1976   *The Hohokam: Desert Farmers & Craftsmen. Excavations at Snaketown, 1964-1965.* University of Arizona Press, Tucson.

Henning, Dale R.
1970   Development and Interrelationships of Oneota Culture in the Lower Missouri River Valley. *Missouri Archaeologist* 32:1-180.

Hibben, Frank C.
1938   A Cache of Wooden Bows from the Mogollon Mountains. *American Antiquity* 4(1):36-38.

1975   *Kiva Art of the Anasazi at Pottery Mound.* KC Publications, Las Vegas.

Hill, W.W.
1982   *An Ethnography of Santa Clara Pueblo, New Mexico.* Edited by Charles H. Lange. University of New Mexico Press, Albuquerque.

Hoefer, Ted, III, Steven D. Creasman, Dirk Murcray, and Joseph Bozovich
1992   The South Baxter Brush Shelter Site: An Early Shoshonean Occupation in Southwest Wyoming. *Wyoming Archaeologist* 36(3-4):47-69.

Hoffman, W.J.
1891   The Midewiwin or "Grand Medicine Society" of the Ojibwa. In *Seventh Annual Report of the Bureau of Ethnology to the Secretary of the Smithsonian Institution, 1885-'86*; pp. 143-300. Washington, D.C.

Hogan, Patrick
1989   Dinetah: A Reevaluation of Pre-Revolt Navajo Occupation in Northwest New Mexico. *Journal of Anthropological Research* 45(1):53-66.

Hoijer, Harry
1956   The Chronology of the Athapaskan Languages. *International Journal of American Linguistics* 22(4):219-232.

Howard, James H.
1953   The Southern Cult in the Northern Plains. *American Antiquity* 19(2):130-138.

1968   *The Southeastern Ceremonial Complex and Its Interpretation.* Memoir No. 6, Missouri Archaeological Society.

Hymes, D.H.
1957   A Note on Athapaskan Glottochronology. *International Journal of American Linguistics* 23(4):291-297.

Jackson, A.T.
1938   *Picture-Writing of Texas Indians.* Anthropological Papers Vol. 2, University of Texas, Austin.

Jelinek, Arthur J.
  1967   *A Prehistoric Sequence in the Middle Pecos Valley, New Mexico.* Anthropological Papers No. 31, Museum of Anthropology, University of Michigan, Ann Arbor.

John, Elizabeth A.H.
  1985   An Earlier Chapter of Kiowa History. *New Mexico Historical Review* 60(4):379-397.

Johnson, Ann M.
  1970a   Montana Projectile Point Types: Avonlea. *Archaeology in Montana* 11(1):45-57.

  1970b   Montana Projectile Point Types: Besant. *Archaeology in Montana* 11(4):55-70.

  1976   Four Petroglyph Sites in Southeastern Montana. *Archaeology in Montana* 17(3):29-42.

Judd, Neil M.
  1926   *Archeological Observations North of the Rio Colorado.* Bureau of American Ethnology Bulletin No. 82. Washington, D.C.

  1954   *The Material Culture of Pueblo Bonito.* Smithsonian Miscellaneous Collections 124. Washington, D.C.

  1959   *Pueblo del Arroyo, Chaco Canyon, New Mexico.* Miscellaneous Collections 138(1). Washington, D.C.

Kelley, J. Charles
  1966   Mesoamerica and the Southwestern United States. In *Handbook of Middle American Indians, Volume 4: Archaeological Frontiers and External Connections*, edited by Gordon F. Ekholm, Gordon R. Willey and Robert Wauchope, pp. 95-110. University of Texas Press, Austin.

Keyser, James D.
  1975   A Shoshonean Origin for the Plains Shield Bearing Warrior Motif. *Plains Anthropologist* 20(69):207-215.

  1977   Writing-On-Stone: Rock Art on the Northwestern Plains. *Canadian Journal of Archaeology* 1:15-80.

  1984   Rock Art of the North Cave Hills. In *Rock Art of Western South Dakota*, edited by L. Adrien Hannus, pp. 1-51. Special Publication No. 9, South Dakota Archaeological Society, Sioux Falls.

Kidder, Alfred Vincent, and Samuel J. Guernsey
1919   *Archeological Explorations in Northeastern Arizona.*   Bureau of American Ethnology Bulletin No. 65. Washington, D.C.

Kingsbury, Lawrence A., and Lorna H. Gabel
1983   Eastern Apache Campsites in Southeastern Colorado: An Hypothesis. In *From Microcosm to Macrocosm: Advances in Tipi Ring Investigation and Interpretation*, edited by Leslie B. Davis, pp. 319-325. Memoir 19, *Plains Anthropologist.*

Kintigh, Keith W.
1985   *Settlement, Subsistence, and Society in Late Zuni Prehistory.* Anthropological Papers of the University of Arizona No. 44. Tucson.

Kluckhohn, Clyde, W.W. Hill, and Lucy Wales Kluckhohn
1971   *Navaho Material Culture.* Belknap Press, Cambridge.

Kroeber, Alfred L.
1902   The Arapaho. *Bulletin of the American Museum of Natural History* 18:1-150.

Lange, Charles H.
1979   Relations of the Southwest with the Plains and Great Basin. In *Handbook of North American Indians, Volume 9: Southwest*, edited by Alfonso Ortiz and William C. Sturtevant, pp. 201-205. Smithsonian Institution, Washington, D.C.

Lewis, T.H.
1889   Stone Monuments in Southern Dakota. *American Anthropologist* (old series) 2(2):159-165.

Lewis, Thomas H.
1985   Bears and Bear Hunting in Prehistory: The Rock Art Record on the Yellowstone. *Northwest Anthropological Research Notes* 19(2):208-245.

1990   The Continuing Use of Petroglyph Sites. *Wyoming Archaeologist* 33(3-4):77-83.

Linati, Claudio
1956   *Trajes Civiles, Militares y Religiosos de Mexico.* Universidad Nacional Autonoma de Mexico, Mexico, D.F.

Loendorf, Lawrence L.
1988   Rock Art Chronology and the Valley of the Shields Site (24CB1094) in Carbon County, Montana. *Archaeology in Montana* 29(2):11-24.

1990   A Dated Rock Art Panel of Shield Bearing Warriors in South Central Montana. *Plains Anthropologist* 35(127):45-54.

Loring, J. Malcolm, and Louise Loring
    1982   *Pictographs and Petroglyphs of the Oregon Country, Part 1: Columbia River and Northern Oregon.* Monograph 21, Institute of Archaeology, University of California, Los Angeles.

Lothson, Gordon Allan
    1976   *The Jeffers Petroglyphs: A Survey and Analysis of the Carvings.* Minnesota Prehistoric Archaeology Series No. 12, Minnesota Historical Society, St. Paul.

Lowrance, Miriam A.
    1986   Rock Art of Northern Brewster County, Texas. *The Artifact* 24(1):1-118.

Lumholtz, Carl
    1902   *Unknown Mexico; A Record of Five Years' Exploration Among the Tribes of the Western Sierra Madre; In the Tierra Caliente of Tepic and Jalisco; And Among the Tarascos of Michoacan.* Two volumes. Charles Scribner's Sons, New York. (Facsimile reprinting by Rio Grande Press, Glorieta, New Mexico, 1973.)

McEwen, Edward, Robert L. Miller, and Christopher A. Bergman
    1991   Early Bow Design and Construction. *Scientific American* 264(6):76-82.

McLeod, C. Milo
    1980   The Lolo Trail: A Significant Travel Route Across the Bitterroots. *Archaeology in Montana* 21(3):117-128.

Magers, Pamela C.
    1986   Miscellaneous Wooden and Vegetal Artifacts. In *Archeological Investigations at Antelope House*, edited by Don P. Morris, pp. 277-305. Publications in Archeology 19, U.S. National Park Service, Washington, D.C.

Magne, Martin P.R., and Michael A. Klassen
    1991   A Multivariate Study of Rock Art Anthropomorphs at Writing-on-Stone, Southern Alberta. *American Antiquity* 56(3):389-418.

Mallery, Garrick
    1893   Picture-Writing of the American Indians. In *Tenth Annual Report of the Bureau of Ethnology to the Secretary of the Smithsonian Institution, 1888-'89.* Washington, D.C.

Martin, Paul S., John B. Rinaldo, and Elaine Bluhm
    1954   *Caves of the Reserve Area.* Fieldiana: Anthropology 42, Chicago Natural History Museum, Chicago.

Martin, Paul S., John B. Rinaldo, Elaine Bluhm, Hugh C. Cutler, and Roger Grange, Jr.
   1952   *Mogollon Cultural Continuity and Change: The Stratigraphic Analysis of Tularosa and Cordova Caves*. Fieldiana: Anthropology 40, Chicago Natural History Museum, Chicago.

Mason, Otis Tufton
   1894   North American Bows, Arrows, and Quivers. In *Annual Report of the Board of Regents of the Smithsonian Institution to July, 1893*, pp. 631-679. Washington, D.C.

Meyer, David
   1988   The Old Women's Phase on the Saskatchewan Plains: Some Ideas. In *Archaeology in Alberta: 1987*, edited by Martin Magne, pp. 55-63. Occasional Paper No. 32, Archaeological Survey of Alberta, Edmonton.

Montgomery, Henry
   1906   Remains of Prehistoric Man in the Dakotas. *American Anthropologist* 8(4):640-651.

Mooney, James
   1898   Calendar History of the Kiowa Indians. In *Seventeenth Annual Report of the Bureau of American Ethnology to the Secretary of the Smithsonian Institution, 1895-96*, pp. 129-445. Washington, D.C.

Morlan, Richard E.
   1988   Avonlea and Radiocarbon Dating. In *Avonlea Yesterday and Today: Archaeology and Prehistory*, edited by Leslie B. Davis, pp. 291-309. Saskatchewan Archaeological Society, Saskatoon.

   1993   A Compendium and Evaluation of Radiocarbon Dates in Saskatchewan. *Saskatchewan Archaeology* 13:3-84.

Morris, Earl H.
   1919   *The Aztec Ruin*. Anthropological Papers of the American Museum of Natural History, 26(1). New York.

   1924   *Burials of the Aztec Ruin*. Anthropological Papers of the American Museum of Natural History, 26(3). New York.

Morris, Earl H., and Robert F. Burgh
   1941   *Anasazi Basketry*. Publication 533, Carnegie Institution of Washington, Washington, D.C.

73

Morris, Elizabeth Ann
1980   *Basketmaker Caves in the Prayer Rock District, Northeastern Arizona.*
        Anthropological Papers of the University of Arizona No. 35. Tucson.

Morss, Noel
1931   *The Ancient Culture of the Fremont River in Utah.* Papers of the Peabody Museum
        of American Archaeology and Ethnology, Harvard University, 12(3). Cambridge.

Mulloy, William
1942   *The Hagen Site.* Publications in the Social Sciences No. 1, University of Montana,
        Missoula.

Newcomb, Franc J., and Gladys A. Reichard
1975   *Sandpaintings of the Navajo Shooting Chant.* Dover Publications, Inc., New York.

Newcomb, W.W., Jr., and Forrest Kirkland
1967   *The Rock Art of Texas Indians.* University of Texas Press, Austin.

Newman, Stanley
1958   *Zuni Dictionary.* Publication 6, Indiana University Research Center, Bloomington.

Nordenskiöld, G.
[1893] *The Cliff Dwellers of the Mesa Verde, Southwestern Colorado: Their Pottery and
        Implements.* P.A. Norstedt & Söner, Stockholm and Chicago.

Nuttall, Zelia
1892   On Ancient Mexican Shields. *Internationales Archiv fur Ethnographie* 5:34-53, 89.

Opler, Morris E.
1941   *An Apache Life-Way: The Economic, Social and Religious Institutions of the
        Chiricahua Indians.* University of Chicago Press.

1983   The Apachean Culture Pattern and Its Origin. In *Handbook of North American
        Indians, Volume 10: Southwest*, edited by Alfonso Ortiz and William C. Sturtevant,
        pp. 368-392. Smithsonian Institution, Washington, D.C.

Parr, Ryan L., Shawn W. Carlyle, and Dennis H. O'Rourke
1996   Ancient DNA Analysis of Fremont Amerindians of the Great Salt Lake Wetlands.
        American Journal of Physical Anthropology 99:507-518.

Peckham, Barbara A.
   1981   Pueblo IV Murals at Mound 7. In *Contributions to Gran Quivira Archeology, Gran Quivira National Monument, New Mexico*, edited by Alden C. Hayes, pp. 165-176. Publications in Archeology 17, U.S. National Park Service, Washington, D.C.

Perry, Richard J.
   1980   The Apachean Transition from the Subarctic to the Southwest. *Plains Anthropologist* 25(90):279-296.

Pettipas, Leo F. (editor)
   1983   *Introducing Manitoba Prehistory*. Popular Series No. 4, Papers in Manitoba Archaeology, Manitoba Department of Cultural Affairs and Historical Resources, Winnipeg.

Proulx, Paul
   1980   The Linguistic Evidence on Algonquian Prehistory. *Anthropological Linguistics* 22(1):1-21.

   1983   The Linguistic Evidence on the Algonquian-Iroquoian Encounter. In *Approaches to Algonquian Archaeology*, edited by Margaret G. Hanna and Brian Kooyman, pp. 189-211. Archaeological Association, University of Calgary, Calgary.

Ray, Verne F.
   1942   *Culture Element Distributions: XXII, Plateau*. University of California Anthropological Records 8(2). Berkeley.

Reed, Alan D., and Jonathon C. Horn
   1990   Early Navajo Occupation of the Southwest: Reexamination of the Dinetah Phase. *Kiva* 55(4):283-300.

Reeves, Brian O.K.
   1983   *Culture Change in the Northern Plains: 1000 B.C.-A.D. 1000*. Occasional Paper No. 20, Archaeological Survey of Alberta, Edmonton.

Renaud, E.B.
   1936   *Pictographs and Petroglyphs of the High Western Plains*. Archaeological Survey Series No. 8, University of Denver, Denver.

Rohn, Arthur H.
   1977   *Cultural Change on Chapin Mesa*. The Regents Press of Kansas, Lawrence.

Russell, Frank
    1908   The Pima Indians. In *Twenty-Sixth Annual Report of the Bureau of American Ethnology to the Secretary of the Smithsonian Institution, 1904-1905*, pp. 3-479. Washington, D.C.

Schaafsma, Polly
    1963   *Rock Art of the Navajo Reservoir District.* Papers in Anthropology No. 7, Museum of New Mexico, Santa Fe.

    1965   Kiva Murals from Pueblo del Encierro (LA 70). *El Palacio* 72(3):7-16.

    1971   *The Rock Art of Utah.* Papers of the Peabody Museum of Archaeology and Ethnology, Harvard University, 65. Cambridge.

    1972   *Rock Art in New Mexico.* State Planning Office, Santa Fe.

    1975   *Rock Art in the Cochiti Reservoir District.* Papers in Anthropology No. 16, Museum of New Mexico, Santa Fe.

    1980   *Indian Rock Art of the Southwest.* School of American Research, Santa Fe and University of New Mexico Press, Albuquerque.

    1992a   Imagery and Magic: Petroglyphs at Comanche Gap, Galisteo Basin, New Mexico. In *Archaeology, Art, and Anthropology: Papers in Honor of J.J. Brody*, edited by Meliha S. Duran and David T. Kirkpatrick, pp. 157-174. The Archaeological Society of New Mexico: 18.

    1992b   *Rock Art in New Mexico.* Revised edition; Museum of New Mexico Press.

Schlesier, Karl H.
    1994   *Plains Indians, A.D. 500-1500: The Archaeological Past of Historic Groups.* University of Oklahoma Press, Norman and London.

Schuster, Helen H.
    1987   Tribal Identification of Wyoming Rock Art: Some Problematic Considerations. *Archaeology in Montana* 28(2):25-43.

Sides, Dorothy Smith
    1961   *Decorative Art of the Southwestern Indians.* Dover Publications, Inc., New York.

Sims, Agnes C.
    1963   Rock Carvings, A Record of Folk History. In *Sun Father's Way: The Kiva Murals of Kuaua*, by Bertha P. Dutton, pp. 214-220. University of New Mexico Press, Albuquerque.

Skeat, Walter W.
1909   *An Etymological Dictionary of the English Language.* Oxford University Press, Oxford.

Smith, Watson
1952   *Kiva Mural Decorations at Awatovi and Kawaika-a, With a Survey of Other Wall Paintings in the Pueblo Southwest.* Papers of the Peabody Museum of American Archaeology and Ethnology, Harvard University, 37. Cambridge.

Smith, Watson, Richard B. Woodbury, and Nathalie F.S. Woodbury
1966   *The Excavation of Hawikuh by Frederick Webb Hodge; Report of the Hendricks-Hodge Expedition, 1917-1923.* Contributions From the Museum of the American Indian, Heye Foundation, 20. New York.

Snow, David H. (editor)
1976   *Archeological Excavations at Pueblo del Encierro, LA 70, Cochiti Dam Salvage Project, Cochiti, New Mexico; Final Report: 1964-1965 Field Seasons.* Lab Notes No. 78, Laboratory of Anthropology, Museum of New Mexico, Santa Fe.

Spier, Leslie
1955   *Mohave Culture Items.* Museum of Northern Arizona Bulletin 28. Flagstaff.

Steed, Paul P.
1980   Rock Art in Chaco Canyon. *The Artifact* 18(3):1-146.

Stevenson, James
1883   Illustrated Catalogue of the Collections Obtained from the Indians of New Mexico and Arizona in 1879. In *Second Annual Report of the Bureau of Ethnology to the Secretary of the Smithsonian Institution, 1880-'81*, pp. 307-422. Washington, D.C.

Stevenson, Matilda Coxe
1904   The Zuni Indians. In *Twenty-Third Annual Report of the Bureau of American Ethnology to the Secretary of the Smithsonian Institution, 1901-1902*, pp. 3-634. Washington, D.C.

Steward, Julian H.
1941   Archeological Reconnaissance of Southern Utah. In *Anthropological Papers, Numbers 13-18*, pp. 275-356. Bureau of American Ethnology Bulletin 128. Washington, D.C.

Stewart, Omer C.
1942   *Culture Element Distributions: XVIII, Ute-Southern Paiute.* University of California Anthropological Records 6(4). Berkeley.

Stirling, Matthew W.
  1942   *Origin Myth of Acoma and Other Records.* Bureau of American Ethnology Bulletin No. 135. Washington, D.C.

Sundstrom, Linea
  1984   The Southern Black Hills. In *Rock Art of Western South Dakota*, edited by L. Adrien Hannus, pp. 53-142. Special Publication No. 9, South Dakota Archaeological Society, Sioux Falls.

Swauger, James L.
  1974   *Rock Art of the Upper Ohio Valley.* Akademische Druck-u. Verlagsanstalt, Graz.

Syms, Leigh
  1977   *Cultural Ecology and Ecological Dynamics of the Ceramic Period in Southwestern Manitoba.* Memoir 12, Plains Anthropologist, Lincoln.

  1979   The Devils Lake-Sourisford Burial Complex on the Northeastern Plains. *Plains Anthropologist* 24(86):283-308.

Turner, Christy G., II
  1963   *Petrographs of the Glen Canyon Region.* Museum of Northern Arizona Bulletin 38. Flagstaff.

Ubelaker, D.H., and R.L. Jantz
  1979   Plains Caddoan Relationships: The View from Craniometry and Mortuary Analysis. *Nebraska History* 60:249-259.

Underhill, Ruth
  1944   *Pueblo Crafts.* U.S. Bureau of Indian Affairs, Washington, D.C.

Vickers, J. Roderick
  1986   *Alberta Plains Prehistory: A Review.* Occasional Paper No. 27, Archaeological Survey of Alberta, Edmonton.

Wade, Edwin L., and Lea S. McChesney
  1981   *Historic Hopi Ceramics: The Thomas V. Keam Collection of the Peabody Museum of Archaeology and Ethnology, Harvard University.* Peabody Museum Press, Cambridge, Massachusetts.

Waring, A.J., Jr., and Preston Holder
  1945   A Prehistoric Ceremonial Complex in the Southeastern United States. *American Anthropologist* 47(1):1-34.

Wasley, William W., and Alfred E. Johnson
 1965   *Salvage Archaeology in Painted Rocks Reservoir, Western Arizona.*
         Anthropological Papers of the University of Arizona No. 9. Tucson.

Wedel, Waldo Randolph
 1936   *An Introduction to Pawnee Archaeology.* Bureau of American Ethnology Bulletin
         112. Washington, D.C.

 1986   *Central Plains Prehistory: Holocene Environments and Culture Change in the
         Republican River Basin.* University of Oklahoma Press, Norman.

Wilcox, David R.
 1981   The Entry of Athapaskans into the American Southwest: The Problem Today. In
         The Protohistoric Period in the North American Southwest, AD 1450 - 1700, edited
         by David R. Wilcox and W. Bruce Masse, pp. 213-256. Arizona State University
         Anthropological Research Papers No. 24. Tempe.

 1988   Avonlea and Southern Athapaskan Migrations. In *Avonlea Yesterday and Today:
         Archaeology and Prehistory,* edited by Leslie B. Davis, pp. 273-280.
         Saskatchewan Archaeological Society, Saskatoon.

Winship, George Parker
 1896   The Coronado Expedition, 1540-1542. In *Fourteenth Annual Report of the Bureau
         of American Ethnology to the Secretary of the Smithsonian Institution, 1892-18,* pp.
         329-613. Washington, D.C.

Wissler, Clark
 1907   *Some Protective Designs of the Dakota.* Anthropological Papers of the American
         Museum of Natural History, 1(2). New York.

 1910   *Material Culture of the Blackfoot Indians.* Anthropological Papers of the American
         Museum of Natural History, 5(1). New York.

Wood, W. Raymond, and Alan S. Downer
 1977   Notes on the Crow-Hidatsa Schism. In *Trends in Middle Missouri Prehistory: A
         Festschrift Honoring the Contributions of Donald J. Lehmer,* edited by W.
         Raymond Wood, pp. 83-100. Memoir 13, Plains Anthropologist, Lincoln.

Wormington, H.M., and Robert H. Lister
 1956   *Archaeological Investigations on the Uncompahgre Plateau.* Proceedings No. 2,
         Denver Museum of Natural History, Denver.

Wright, Barton
    1976   *Pueblo Shields from the Fred Harvey Fine Arts Collection.* Northland Press, Flagstaff.

Young, Robert W., and William Morgan
    1980   *The Navajo Language.* University of New Mexico Press, Albuquerque.

www.ingramcontent.com/pod-product-compliance
Lightning Source LLC
Chambersburg PA
CBHW081519040426
42447CB00013B/3272